Practical Treatment in Psychiatry

EDITED BY

J.L.CRAMMER

Consultant Psychiatrist,
St. John's Hospital,
Stone, Aylesbury

BLACKWELL SCIENTIFIC PUBLICATIONS

OXFORD AND EDINBURGH

SBN 632 05440 9

FIRST PUBLISHED 1968

Printed in Great Britain by
THE SALISBURY PRESS LTD
SALISBURY
and bound by
THE KEMP HALL BINDERY, OXFORD

Contents

Foreword

This book represents the substance of a three-day course held at New College, Oxford, 27-29 March 1968, under the auspices of the Committee for Postgraduate Medical Studies of the University. The course was planned primarily for the benefit of those beginning specialisation in psychiatry and likely to sit a D.P.M. examination, and the emphasis was on drugs and simple procedures applicable without special training. This is the sense of the word 'practical' in the title of the book. Most of the chapters deal with the treatment of common categories of patients referred to hospitals and specialist clinics and what housemen or registrars may do about them, but the underlying general principles and the scientific validity of treatments are stressed throughout. The emphasis is on this rational approach, and on recent progress, and no attempt has been made to be comprehensive or exhaustive, which would have been impossible in the time and space allowed.

Effective treatment in psychiatry is largely the result of recent discoveries which are having an increasing influence on general practice and public health. Chapters of this book may therefore be useful to practitioners who want to know something of what psychiatry can offer their patients, and to community care workers faced with the problems posed by epileptics, alcoholics or chronic psychotics in everyday life.

We are grateful to all those who helped in the organisation of the course, to the chairmen of the sessions, to the speakers who also wrote their lectures, and to the editor and publishers

of *Hospital Medicine* for permission to reprint the article by
Dr Griffith Edwards in place of the unscripted talk given by him.

J.L.C.
F.E.K.
D.C.W.

The Oxford Scheme for
Postgraduate Training in Psychiatry

Until recently organized postgraduate training in psychiatry did not exist in the Oxford region. Instruction was limited to the supervision of trainee psychiatrists by consultants, with case discussions and occasional lectures. A few trainees were also able to attend the courses of lectures at the Maudsley Hospital, London, but the great amount of time spent in travelling back and forth was uneconomic. There was in addition an occasional privately organised residential course held in Oxford.

Five years ago representatives of the six psychiatric hospitals—Borocourt, Fair Mile, Littlemore, St Crispin's, St John's and Warneford—and of the University of Oxford met under the guidance of Dr A.W.Williams, the University's Director of Postgraduate Studies, and a committee for postgraduate training in psychiatry was set up. Professor G.W.Harris F.R.S. agreed to organize a ten-day course annually in neuro-anatomy and neuro-physiology, Professor Ritchie Russell and Dr Charles Whitty to accept trainee psychiatrists from the Region for a six-week secondment to the department of clinical neurology at the teaching hospitals in Oxford, and Dr May Davidson to organize psychology seminars. In addition three times a year a three-day lecture course was to be held, sometimes in one of the hospitals, sometimes in a centre in the University, each with a primary theme drawn from the field of study of psychiatry necessary for the examination for a Diploma in Psychological Medicine but treated in a broad enough way to be a refresher course also for consultants.

All these training facilities have now been successfully in operation for some time. All are open to all trainee psychiatrists in the Region without cost to themselves. The present work represents the substance of one three-day course, but others have been held on geriatrics, subnormality, forensic psychiatry, child psychiatry, psychosomatic medicine, social psychiatry, managing to cover in the process such diverse themes as genetics, therapeutic abortion, childhood autism, confusional states, suicide, affective disorders in the aged, electroencephalography and so on. Some of the speakers have been distinguished visitors, some from the University and the Region.

Latterly the organization of training has been strengthened by the appointment of area tutors in each hospital and of a Regional Adviser for Postgraduate Education in Psychiatry to organize and coordinate the various programmes. Day-release schemes of training, already successful in psychology, are to be extended. With the imminent creation of a University department of Psychiatry the regional organization of training in this speciality will be close to that recommended in the recent report of the Royal Commision on Medical Education.

David C. Watt
Regional Adviser for
Postgraduate Education in Psychiatry.

The Authors

GRIFFITH EDWARDS M.A. D.M. D.P.M. Honorary Consultant Psychiatrist and Senior Lecturer, Institute of Psychiatry, Maudsley Hospital, London

M.G.GELDER M.A. D.M. M.R.C.P. D.P.M. formerly Senior Lecturer, Institute of Psychiatry, Maudsley Hospital, London; now Professor of Psychiatry, Oxford

F.J.J.LETEMENDIA M.D. D.P.M. Consultant Psychiatrist, Littlemore Hospital, Oxford

D.V.PARKE B.SC. PH.D. F.R.I.C. Professor of Biochemistry, University of Surrey, London, S.W.11

D.M.SHAW M.B. B.S. PH.D. M.R.C.P. a member of the Neuropsychiatric Research Unit of the Medical Research Council, Carshalton, Surrey

MICHAEL SHEPHERD M.A. D.M. M.R.C.P. D.P.M. Professor of Epidemiological Psychiatry, Institute of Psychiatry, Maudsley Hospital, London

ANDREW SODDY M.A. M.B. B.CHIR. D.P.M. Senior Registrar at St. John's Hospital, Stone, Aylesbury

D.C.TAYLOR M.B. D.P.M. Medical Research Officer at the Human Development Research Unit, and Honorary Consultant Psychiatrist, Park Hospital for Children, Oxford

D.C.WATT B.SC. M.D. D.P.M. Medical Director, St. John's Hospital, Stone, Aylesbury, and Regional Adviser for Postgraduate Education in Psychiatry, Oxford

J.H.WILLIS M.B. M.R.C.P. ED. D.P.M. Consultant Psychiatrist in Drug Addiction to Guy's, King's College, and Bexley Hospitals, London

Treatment of drug addiction

J. H. WILLIS

Guy's, King's College and
Bexley Hospitals, London

J. H. WILLIS

Guy's, King's College and
Bexley Hospitals, London

INTRODUCTION

The study of the treatment of drug addiction shows that this is a treatment area where the failure rate is high. Commonly the expectation of failure is such and the zeal of both medical and nursing personnel so blunted by repeated lack of success that the problems tend to be approached with wary cynicism.

Of course the problems are complex, involving physiological, pharmacological and social factors, and while space cannot permit examination of these in any detail here it is neccessary to stress their existence when postulating a model of addiction useful in planning treatment. For too long there has been a tendency to apply over-simplistic approaches.

The word 'addiction' presents difficulties in definition. For this reason, in its 13th report the W.H.O. Expert Committee on Addiction-producing drugs (1964) recommended the term 'dependence' instead :

> 'Drug dependence is a state of psychic or physical dependence or both, on a drug, arising in a person following administration of that drug on a periodic or continuous basis. The characteristics must always be made clear by designating the particular type of drug dependence in each case; for example drug dependence of morphine type, of barbiturate type, of amphetamine type, etc.'

This provides a basis for the identification of patterns of drug usage and emphasizes that they will vary from one drug to

1

another. Previously it was customary to categorize all forms of drug dependence under the collective term 'drug addiction' as if they were all similar and simply an expression of the equation drug + patient = addiction, which they are not.

Table 1 displays briefly the varieties of physical and psychological dependence associated with the important drugs of addiction. Obviously drugs which produce intense dependence will present special problems in withdrawal.

TABLE 1.

Drug	Physical Dependence	Psychological Dependence
Opiates	Always present	Always present
Barbiturates	Only develops if dosage maintained well above usual therapeutic levels	Varies enormously tends to be intermittent
Amphetamines	None	Variable
Cocaine	None	Marked
Cannabis (marihuana)	None	Variable

The extent of the drug problem in Britain has been reviewed by Bewley (1966) and some of his figures are displayed in Table 2.

TABLE 2. Estimate of incidence of drug misuse in U.K. 1966. (T.H. Bewley)

Drug	Rate per 100,000 of population
Hallucinogens	1
Cocaine	1-3
Morphine/Heroin	4-5
Cannabis	30-60
Amphetamines	100-200 Slight dependency-prescribed 100-200 illicit use
Barbiturates	150-250 Regular use, dependent 800-1200 Regular use, not dependent

Present concern in this country centres on the abuse of opiates and for this reason the present paper focuses on opiates—heroin particularly. But it cannot be too strongly emphasized that heroin addiction is but one aspect of the larger area of drug or substance abuse. It is vital to pay more attention to the drug users than to the substances themselves.

A model of heroin addiction

Chein *et al* (1964) have produced a rational and meaningful model of heroin addiction which can be applied to addictive states in general. In a research enquiry into heroin usage amongst youngsters in New York City they postulate criteria of addiction including

1. psychological $\begin{cases} \text{craving} \\ \text{close personal involvement with drug usage} \end{cases}$
dependence
2. physical dependence

Craving may relate to physical dependence but is not necessarily an expression of its presence—it is a phenomenon that may be remarkably unpredictable in intensity and one which can wreck an apparently successful treatment programme in a given case. Close personal involvement with drug use refers to the radical alterations in life style that so often accompany addiction. The addict adopts new habits of living, enters a subculture and identifies and proclaims himself as a member of it by behaviour, appearance, dress and language. If this subculture attracts hostility he is likely to confirm the negative expectations of society and increase his own level of anomic social withdrawal. If the society concerned imposes direct sanctions on drug usage, as in the U.S.A., then the addict will move further into antisocial attitudes and acts, plus criminal activity to support an illegal drug habit.

It seems likely that in heroin addiction, while physical dependence is invariably present, psychological dependence may have important ramifications which can materially affect treatment. Perhaps it is a failure to recognise this that may account for some of the poor results of treatment to date. Finally it should be emphasised that addiction does not arise independently of psychiatric pathology. Addicts predominantly are people with major personality disorders.

Goals of treatment in heroin addiction

Traditional medical treatment offers total abstention as the primary treatment goal in all cases. When it is realised that in many follow-up studies a relapse rate of the order of 90% (Hunt and Odoroff 1962) is seen in the first six months after discharge it may be thought that such a goal is unrealistic in every case. Rather one should aim to assess the primary treatment needs of each patient, recognising the different patterns of the natural history of addiction that may exist. Thus it should be possible to plan a treatment programme for each patient according to his needs rather than imposing the same rigid treatment schedule for everyone. It is this over-simple rigidity which has hampered the proper study of these problems to date.

PRINCIPLES AND METHODS OF TREATMENT
(1) Withdrawal

Withdrawal from heroin or any opiate is not ordinarily a difficult procedure providing a few general principles are observed. In the first place it can only satisfactorily be carried out in hospital under careful nursing observation. The method described here is not suggested as the ideal, merely as an approach which the author has found is workable in practice. It depends primarily on the use of methadone 'physeptone' as a substitute drug. Methadone is a synthetic analgesic which has a longer duration of action than heroin and which has the basic property of cross-tolerance so that it can be used in all forms of opiate withdrawal.

Since addicts commonly overstate their drug consumption it is useful to wait for signs of moderate withdrawal distress (Table 3) before commencing medication.

TABLE 3. Opiate abstinence syndrome

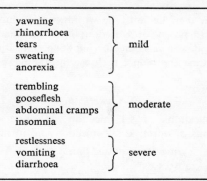

yawning rhinorrhoea tears sweating anorexia	mild
trembling gooseflesh abdominal cramps insomnia	moderate
restlessness vomiting diarrhoea	severe

In practice it is possible to offer the patient intramuscular injections of heroin during the first three days. These may be given thrice daily, starting off with one half or one third of the dose the patient has been having outside hospital. The dose is halved on three successive days and then stopped. When combined with oral methadone twice daily the withdrawal distress is not great and the methadone may then be reduced and withdrawn in the following week. It should be emphasised that the patient has to accept some distress. In a sense if withdrawal distress does not occur then the drug is not being withdrawn. Phenothiazines and other tranquilisers though commonly prescribed are strictly speaking not necessary. Their usefulness has never clearly been demonstrated with opiate withdrawal and they do carry the potential hazard of precipitating with-

drawal fits if the patient has been medicating himself with barbiturates.

Insomia may be troublesome and is best dealt with using
non-barbiturate hypnotics. Since multiple drug consumption
is common a history of barbiturate consumption should always
be enquired after. This is important since barbiturate withdrawal
complicated by fits and states of delirium is a hazardous clinical
problem. If the patient is showing evidence of chronic barbiturate
intoxication then he must be withdrawn gradually from barbiturates. In practice this is done by re-intoxicating him to a
state where he shows slight slurring of speech. It is safest to use
pentobarbitone and reduce the dose by 100 mg. per day.

(2) *Complications*

The complications of self-injection with heroin are mainly
complications of unsterile self-injection and include:—

> syringe-transmitted jaundice
> abscesses
> septicaemia
> endocarditis
> thrombophlebitis
> pneumonia
> overdosage

These will be dealt with using primary medical methods and
it should be emphasized that these complications are common
and highly relevant.

> e.g. A 22 year old girl was attending the clinic and receiving
> prescriptions for heroin. On the morning she was due to
> attend the clinic a casualty officer at a hospital on the other
> side of London telephoned to say she was 'in withdrawal dis-
> tress and making a lot of noise.' He gave her physeptone and
> sent her to the clinic in the afternoon. When seen in the am-
> bulance she was near-moribund. On admission to a general

hospital she was found to have extensive pneumonia with neck stiffness. It took three weeks for her temperature to return to normal. She survived.

During the withdrawal period the patient's physical status can be assessed and investigations, including tests of liver function, carried out.

(3) *Abstention—general measures*

The goal of maintained abstention is notoriously difficult to attain. For this reason it is not possible to do more than indicate approaches aimed at rehabilitation of the addict. In the first place it should be recognised that the addict who has developed close personal involvement with drug usage and the addict sub-culture is likely to need dramatic reorientation of his social values and attitudes if he is to abandon drug taking. Since the activity of drug getting and the involvement in drug usage will have become central areas of his life experience the task of altering this necessarily presents a formidable problem. This would be hard enough in a non-deviant subject but when one adds to this the fact that addiction so commonly occurs with social deviancy and major personality disorder, the extent of the task becomes apparent.

Psychotherapy, whether in a group or individual setting, is therefore difficult. One of the major tasks is to get the patients to talk about subjects other than drugs. Having taken this first step it is then necessary to use psychotherapeutic endeavour to alter the addict's view of himself and the world and to see his drug-taking as it really is. Addicts frequently use drugs almost like analgesics to avoid primary areas of distress and to diminish primary needs (Wikler 1953) and any successful psychotherapy must enable the patient to live in the world as it is. 'Rehabilit-ation' and 'treatment' therefore become almost indistinguishable terms. In Britain long-term rehabilitation schemes are virtually only at drawing board stage but it is possible to learn from U.S.

experience where notable rehabilitation facilities for addicts have been developed.

Synanon was started in California by a former alcoholic. It is a structured community in which ex-addicts occupy a senior position in the hierarchy. The addict enters such a community at the lower end of the social order and is exposed to vigorous group interaction of a fairly authoritarian variety. Entry to the community is in a sense made difficult so that the best motivated addicts are most likely to be accepted.

Daytop Lodge, started by a former Synanon member, utilises rational authority in a more open community and has achieved impressive results as a model of rehabilitation. Again group interaction is used and the addict is exposed to the re-educative experiences of former addicts. These approaches are essentially reality based and seek to influence deviant behaviours by community influences. The Daytop Lodge milieu appears to offer a most promising setting for rehabilitating an addict. As yet facilities of this sort are not available in Britain. Daytop is certainly a model that one would like to see copied.

(4) *Absention—pharmacological aids*

A. *Methadone maintenance*

Dole and Nyswander (1966) have demonstrated the blockade effect of methadone in high dosage. It is used as an anti-narcotic agent—not as a substitute for heroin. The object is to prevent the euphoriant action of heroin, by gradually building up a once daily dose till pharmacological blockade is achieved.

The rationale is that the heroin addict rarely feels that he is functioning normally—to use addict jargon 'straight'. Owing to his tolerance and the speed of action of heroin he veers quickly between withdrawal distress ('sick') and euphoria ('high'). This state of fluctuant intoxication added to his personality disorder makes his chances of keeping a job, or even wanting to, minimal.

Methadone maintenance helps him to function normally, i.e. to feel 'straight' and to behave in a socially productive fashion.

The dosage of methadone is commenced in hospital. During this stage (six weeks) the object is to build up the daily dose to a level of between 100–300 mg per day in one dose. In practice it has been found that the blockade effect is produced at this level. It is usually best to start off with a twice-daily dose, gradually reducing the second dose and spilling it over into the first. Unwanted side effects are met by dose reduction and awaiting further tolerance. The *Side effects* include :

> drowsiness
> vomiting and nausea
> sweating
> obesity (not severe)
> delayed or absent orgasm.

The drug is best administered in liquid form. In New York they have found that the intramuscular preparation is suitable by mouth in fruit juice. Alternatively elixir methadone may be used. After leaving hospital the patient calls every day for his daily dose of methadone. The Methadone Maintenance Program in New York has been successful in the treatment of addicts with a known history of addiction of more than five years' duration in whom repeated treatment failures had been reported.

It might be said that such patients are at a stage in their addictive career when they are ready to mature out of their habit (Winick 1962) or when they may have achieved a higher degree of motivation to abstain. However it is a fact that in 1967 Dole and Nyswander had reported 400 patients as being in the programme and 60% of them were working. The failure rate was of the order of 10%. Such results are encouraging, to say the least.

B. *Cyclazocine*

Cyclazocine is an orally effective morphine antagonist which has a long duration of action. It is a drug of the benzomorphan series. When given it impedes the direct pharmacological actions of opiates and, which is perhaps more important, prevents their subjective effects so that the patient experiences no 'high' if he should inject himself with an opiate. This suggests a way of extinguishing the conditioned physical dependence that is an important aspect of addiction. Clinical experience often reveals patients who have withdrawal symptoms long after their pharmacological dependence is finished. Such symptoms may be evoked by situations associated with drug-taking. Conditioned abstinence symptoms have also been produced in animals using etonitazine (Wikler et al 1962),

Jaffe (1966) and Freedman (1967) report experiences with the use of cyclazocine in addicts. In Freedman's series of 52 patients it proved possible to maintain 30 in a regular treatment situation. Martin and Grodetsky (1967) report an intensive study of 6 patients maintained on cyclazocine. Admittedly experience of cyclazocine is as yet limited, but it is a pharmacological approach with important possibilities.

(5) *Maintenance prescription of heroin*

This is a treatment method which needs to be evaluated. The 'British system' of prescribing for addicts worked well when addicts were 'therapeutic' in origin, middle-aged, and not members of a subculture. But the present situation is entirely different and there is no doubt that prescribing has been misused.

The object of prescribing heroin is to give the patient sufficient heroin to avoid withdrawal distress, not make him 'high'. As heroin acts quickly this is difficult and it is not clear whether the method is applicable to all patients.

It should be made clear to patients that maintenance

prescriptions of opiates is not a treatment goal in itself but that nevertheless it can be used as an opportunity for the patient to put his trust in the doctor: something that hitherto he may have been unable to do for a variety of reasons. Thus it may be possible to lead him to a more productive treatment situation. It has to be conceded however that many patients regard the prescription of heroin as being the primary treatment method and are not interested in abstention. This is very common in young addicts who have not become fully aware of the real hazards of addiction and who may hardly recognise themselves as such. This undoubtedly raises basic problems in the doctor-patient relationship since often the patient's behaviour and attitudes towards the doctor will be primarily motivated by his desire to receive heroin. The most difficult task is to assess how much heroin should be prescribed. In fact the only satisfactory way to assess a patient's needs is by admission to hospital for observation for 72 hours where he can be stabilised on a minimal dose of heroin. However, few patients will agree to this and in most cases addicts overstate their needs for a variety of reasons.

High doses of heroin, i.e. anything in excess of 240 mg heroin per day, are very difficult to stabilise since this amount of heroin does not merely control withdrawal distress but is likely to produce states of 'high' and an increasing demand for the drug. In fact this is one of the central problems of maintenance prescription. How can one stabilise a deviant person on an intoxicating drug which produces an increasing subjective need for its use ?

It is to be hoped that this question will be answered with the hospital-based centres which follow the Dangerous Drugs Act of 1967. This places the onus of maintenance prescribing on licensed doctors and presents an opportunity once and for all to evaluate whether or not prescribing drugs works. It also gives an opportunity to learn something of the natural history of patients receiving such prescriptions.

SUMMING UP

In Western Society opiates generally are regarded with disfavour outside their strictly medical uses and society places sanctions on their illicit use. In the United States the sanctions are direct and clearly defined, in Britain they are indirect. Popular and for that matter medical stereotypes of the heroin addict are likely to be influenced by fiction and plain lack of experience rather than fact. For a variety of reasons heroin addicts may evoke strong negative feelings on the part of doctors and nurses. These feelings may have both to do with the life style of addicts, the poor results of treatment, and a general feeling of helplessness experienced in the face of a phenomenon that is inexplicable, persistent, and often wearisome. The same comments could be made about many chronic disorders but addiction is peculiar in that it is a disorder that the individual may appear to have selected. It should be noted too that addicts may evoke positive feelings in the inexperienced—and these reactions can be equally misleading.

The deleterious effects of heroin are more properly the affects of unsterile injections than of heroin itself while the effects on the addicts' social behaviour tend to render him passive rather than actively anti-social. He and society usually suffer or are made aware of his existence when he is without the drug. It has often been said that the alcoholic suffers when he is intoxicated, the addict when he is not. One of the basic problems appears to be that for a wide range of reasons—some of them obvious some not—people choose to intoxicate themselves periodically or continuously. Depending on what culture they live in their intoxication is either tolerated or proscribed.

When someone becomes an addict or is defined as such it is customary to offer total abstention as a basic treatment goal. In the case of heroin addiction this is extremely difficult since the majority of addicts return to drug use, and there is as yet no treatment method which is better than any other in favouring abstention. The history of the treatment of opiate addiction is marked by frequent (later unsubstantiated) claims of dramatic success. Yet constantly the demand for such success persists. It has to be asked not whether total abstinence is a reasonable goal but rather whether it is a reasonable goal for every patient. Because of the urgency of the problem there is an unscientific tendency to try and develop a treatment modality applicable to all cases.

If addiction were a one-factor state this would be acceptable. But it is not. It would seem logical then to approach the problem by concentrating not just on the addict or just on the drug but rather by evaluating the total situation: examining the natural history of the addict's drug usage without any preconceived notions. In this way differing patterns of drug use may be recognised, compared with one another, and evaluated against the background of the patient's life situation and development. There is a need for a return to traditional medical and psychiatric practice in this respect. Each patient needs to be assessed in a climate of clinical enquiry uninfluenced by the demands of tenuous theory.

Finally it should be emphasised that addiction is rarely confined to one drug. The use of methylamphetamine administered by self-injection shows a continuing increase, with states of severe psychological dependence. This has been demonstrated by recent experience in Sweden where methylamphetamime addiction is the most prevalent form of drug abuse by young people. It is worth noting that prescribing clinics were tried in this instance and were not successful.

It is evident too that further changes may be imminent in British type of drug abuse. In the U.S.A. for instance the number of heroin addicts though large is relatively static, though the middle and upper class white addict is now becoming more common. But the abuse of amphetamines and marijuana shows a rapid increase among young Americans. What are the implications of this? If 70% of a population is smoking marijuana does marijuana smoking then become a normal activity?

We face a continuing increase in opiate and soft drug abuse, there is little doubt of this. The present function of treatment units is thus to collect information while offering treatment possibilities, clear in aim and explicit in intention. There must be no suggestion that a treatment unit offers solutions to complex problems, no matter how strong the pressures may be.

REFERENCES

BEWLEY T. H. (1966) Recent changes in patterns of drug addiction in the United Kingdom. *Bull. Narcotics*, **18**, 4, 1-13.

CHEIN I., GERARD D. L., LEE R. S. and ROSENFELD E. (1964) *Narcotics Delinquency and Social Policy-the road to H.* New York, Basic Books.

DOLE V. P., NYSWANDER M. and KREEK M. J. (1966) Narcotic blockade *Arch. Intern. Med.* **118**, 304-309.

FREEDMAN A. M. (1967) Experiences with cyclazocine. Paper presented at *Symposium on Drug Addiction.* London Committee, Society for Study of Addiction.

HUNT G. H. and ODOROFF M. E. (1962) Follow-up studies of narcotics addicts after hospitalisation *U.S. Pub. Health. Repts.* **77**, 41.

JAFFE J. H. and BRILL L. (1966) Cyclazocine; a long acting narcotic antagonist. Its voluntary acceptance as a treatment modality by narcotic addicts. *Int. J. Addict.* **1**, 99-123.

MARTIN W. R. and GRODETSKY C. W. (1967) Cyclazocine, an adjunct in the treatment of narcotic addiction. *Int J, Addict.* **2**, 85-93.

WIKLER A. (1953) *Opiate Addiction: psychological and neurophysiological aspects in relation to clinical problems.* Thomas, Springfield Illinois.

WIKLER A., MARTIN W. R., PESCOR F. T. and EADES G. (1962) Factors regulating oral consumption of Etonitazine solution by Morphine-addicted rats. *Pharmacologist*, **4**, 154.

WINICK C. (1962) Maturing out of narcotic addiction. *Bull. Narcotics U.N. Dept. Social Affairs.* **14**, 1.

Treatment of Alcoholism

GRIFFITH EDWARDS

Institute of Psychiatry,
Maudsley Hospital, London

'Every morning when I woke up I was sick, I was ill. My hands were so shaky that I'd have to lift that first drink to my lips very, very carefully to make sure it wasn't spilled. I'd be in such a nervous state that when I got to the pub I'd sit at the bar and have the first drink while staring in the mirror to make sure no one would come up behind me suddenly. Butterflies in the stomach! Sometimes in the morning the sweat would be pouring off me, and when I woke up I'd have the heaves so that even cleaning my teeth would make me retch. I had so many terrible fears—I'd even been afraid to cross over a bridge. Those horrible feelings in the morning, but all I needed was a couple of drinks to cure me. Sometimes I'd have a bottle in my room sometimes I'd be off to one of the early morning market pubs. Ten minutes after that first drink I'd start to feel myself coming right. I suppose I was getting through a bottle and a half of whisky most days. Provided I kept myself topped up I was all right. I tell you, all those years I didn't think about much else other than where the next drink was coming from. Slip out in lunch hour. Keep a bottle in the office. I would go into a pub on the way home meaning to have just a couple of drinks but I wouldn't be home till closing time—I was past the stage of being able to drink like a normal person. And really, towards the end, I wasn't even getting any pleasure from the stuff but I just had to keep drinking.'

THE MEANING OF DEPENDENCE

Habituation, addiction, dependence

Dependence is as real and important a phenomenon as the obsessional symptom, and like the obsession it is remarkably difficult to define. This paper is concerned not with the peripheral problems of treating the host of physical, psychological and social symptoms which follow in the wake of dependence-drinking, but with the treatment of the central illness, a man's developing a state in which drinking, rather than being a take-it-or-leave-it affair, appears to him to have become a dominating necessity, a dependence from which he cannot, without help, break.

In the past, an effort was made to distinguish between 'habituation' and 'addiction' but the logical basis on which this distinction was drawn was never satisfactory. The World Health Organisation subsequently proposed (W.H.O. 1964) that rather than attempt to maintain two separate categories of drug abuse the more useful approach was to recognise that every drug produces its own syndrome of dependence. With some drugs physiological dependence may dominate the picture, while with others only psychological dependence can be demonstrated. Seeing the dependency syndromes as a family of diseases, which may often have something in common but which do not conform to any one stereotype, is more useful than employing as previously a typology which set up the stereotype of narcotic dependence as true addiction: this stereotype encouraged the neglect of substances such as alcohol and barbiturates which do not conform to the chosen picture.

Analysing dependence

Analysing the relative contributions of psychological and physiological factors in any particular dependency syndrome is a difficult matter, but this analysis is obviously of great importance to further understanding of drug and alcohol abuse. Attempts have been made to explain alcohol dependence within a psychoanalytical, a learning theory, or a physiological model.

Views on the psychopathology of alcoholism began to be formulated fairly early in the history of the analytical movement and the contribution of the analysts to the understanding of alcoholism has since been the subject of two extensive reviews (Lorand, 1945; Blum, 1966). The one common feature of all the analytical explanations is the postulate that excessive drinking is merely a symptom of the underlying personality disturbance which must be the true concern of the therapist: alcohol dependence has variously been interpreted as a manifestation of oral dependence, latent homosexuality and a subconscious drive towards self-destruction. Today probably most analysts would be reluctant to offer any one overall explanation of the psychopathology of alcoholism, but would wish rather to make their contribution by exploring the dynamics of the dependence in the individual case.

A learning theory model has been proposed by a number of different authors (Kepner, 1964), but so far the formulations offered have not been worked out in much detail. Alcohol is seen as producing pleasant physiologically-induced states of feeling which are their own immediate reward, as well as drink giving relief from unpleasant states of anxiety, tension and guilt. Each time the patient takes a drink the reward reinforces his drinking behaviour but why every ordinary person, or at least every anxious person, does not escalate from social drinking to alcohol dependence is clearly not explained by so simplistic a formulation. It seems however likely that learning theories have here an important contribution to make—it is possible that the fact that for the alcohol-dependent person one drink is often inexorably followed by another until a certain state of intoxication is reached is in part a phenomenon which can be regarded as 'learnt' behaviour.

The physiological theory of alcohol dependence is the model which is at present backed by the best experimental evidence. The debate as to whether alcohol is a drug capable of producing physiological dependence—whether in terms of the old nomenclature it is 'truly an addictive drug'—was settled when Isbell et al. (1955) gave large quantities of alcohol (266-489 ml. of 95% ethyl alcohol per day) to 10 ex-morphine addict volunteers for periods ranging from seven to 87 days. Four patients who dropped out relatively early in the experiment exhibited, on cessation of drinking, mild and brief symptoms of tremulousness, nausea, perspiration and insomnia but the six patients who drank for 48 or more days showed on cessation varieties of severe withdrawal phenomena—two had epiletic seizures and three had frank delirium tremens—and this despite an adequate diet and multiple vitamin supplements throughout the period of intoxication. More recently a very detailed series of psychophysiological, psychiatric and biochemical observations has been made on a group of 10 volunteers who ingested large quantities of whisky for 24 days and were then withdrawn—tremor, disorientation, amnesias and hallucinations occurred in eight of the 10 subjects.

Although the reality of alcohol's ability to produce a physiologically based withdrawal syndrome is no longer to be doubted, whether prolonged exposure to alcohol in high doses produces an irreversible metabolic lesion which then dictates that the person will inevitably return to abnormal drinking if he attempts social drinking is a question still open to investigation. That a few drinks lead to dramatic relapse could be as much a matter of the underlying psychopathology or of some conditioning process as of an acquired metabolic error.

Establishing the diagnosis

Whatever the conflicting theories on the basis of the dependent state there are in practice a number of symptoms which the alcohol-dependent patient reports, and it is on the elicitation of these that the diagnosis is made. The quotation which started this paper gave a picture of dependence in severe and advanced form: the syndrome is not however an all-or-none phenomenon. The symptoms to be looked for are as follows:

1. The subjective experience that drinking cannot be controlled, that alcohol is causing damage but cannot be left alone, that drinking like a normal person is no longer possible.

2. Amnesias. Blackouts may certainly occur in normal people who have drunk intemperately, but frequent experience of blackouts is unusual other than at levels of drinking which imply dependency or carry the risk of dependency developing. Amnesias occurring during the day and alcohol fugues are a more advanced symptom than the familiar loss of memory for the night before.

3. Withdrawal symptoms. Because alcohol is a short-acting drug only a few hours of abstinence are necessary for these symptoms to be brought on, and they typically occur on waking. Nausea and 'heaves', sweatiness, anxiety and mild tremors are the first symptoms to make their appearance, and if the patient is severely chemically dependent and if these symptoms are not relieved by further drinking then they may progress to something more major—severe shakes and severe anxiety, transient confusion and transient visual and auditory hallucinations, and finally delirium tremors or alcohol-withdrawal fits.

4. Craving. This term is really used to describe two different phenomena. The patient during the acute withdrawal phase experiences craving because he knows that a further drink will relieve his unpleasant symptoms. When he has recovered from the withdrawal phase he will no longer have this sort of craving and patients at this point declare that because all craving has gone they cannot possibly be diagnosed as alcohol-dependent. Rarely, the patient will continue to complain that he is still continuously obsessed by thoughts of drink, but much more often during the first weeks or months of recovering he will

report that craving returns intermittently, and specially at moments of stress or upset—this sort of episode has been referred to as 'a dry drunk'.

5.   Beverage choice. The alcohol-dependent person may continue to drink nothing but whisky or beer, but a useful pointer to the diagnosis is his having changed his habits to drinking forms of alcohol which are indicative of a need to obtain the maximum alcohol for the minimum expenditure. Rough cider, and British wine, and surgical or methylated spirits are likely choices.

6.   Damage. Someone may certainly incur physical, social or mental damage as a result of drinking without his being dependent on alcohol. To take an obvious example a man may simply get drunk and fall down stairs. But by and large the more evidence of varieties of damage, the more the patient seems to be continuing his heavy drinking despite the accumulation of obvious pain and suffering which would be expected to make him moderate his drinking, the more likely is he to be dependent.

A useful procedure in history taking, and one which covers enquiry into most of the points mentioned above, is with the patient's assistance to reconstruct (hour by hour) a *typical drinking day*, starting with how the patient feels when he wakes up and then working through where he drinks, what he drinks and how much he drinks during the course of the whole day. For instance, how long is spent in the pub at lunch time, how much in terms of doubles and singles is drunk during that period? It is useless to ask at the outset for such overall information as the total daily alcohol consumption—the accurate picture is only likely to emerge from careful and detailed questioning.

Alcohol dependence and other types of alcoholism

As mentioned above not every person who is drinking excessively is dependent on alcohol. Whether the term 'alcoholism' is applied only when dependence can be demonstrated or whether on the other hand the use of the word is broadened to include all cases in which drink is causing damage is an important matter for definition.   Sadly confusion reigns, with different authorities using the word in different ways.

The most widely accepted definition is that offered by the World Health Organisation (1951) and here dependence is one of the clauses.

> 'Alcoholics are those excessive drinkers whose dependence on alcohol has attained such a degree that they show a noticeable mental disturbance or an interference with their mental and bodily health their interspersonal relations and their smooth social and economic functioning or who show the prodromal signs of such development.'

Another approach to the problems of definition and classification which has been influential is that contained in Jellinek's classical work 'The Disease Concept of Alcoholism'. He proposed that alcoholism could be seen as comprising five syndromes:

Alpha. '. . . a purely psychological continual dependence or reliance upon alcohol to relieve bodily or emotional pain.'

Beta. Those drinkers who cause themselves physical damage such as cirrhosis, but who do not show evidence of dependence.

Gamma. The classical picture of loss of control, withdrawal symptoms and adaptive metabolism.

Delta. The patient is again dependent, but here the hallmark is not loss of control but inability to abstain: drinking is not chaotic or necessarily even at all socially disruptive. A typical example is the Frenchman who is leading a normally adjusted life but is a very heavy wine drinker—when for some reason he suddenly has to stop drinking, to everyone's surprise he develops delirium tremens.

Epsilon. The bout drinker, or dipsomaniac.

Whatever the virtues of the various exact definitions which have been propounded the fact probably remains that in the majority of published clinical and research reports the term alcoholism has been used with no precision at all, and we have to accept that the only way to interpret the great bulk of the literature is to regard the alcoholic as broadly comprising every type of pathological drinker or problem drinker.

The designation alcohol dependence or alcohol addiction seems however to have been a term used with more consistency. It would be wrong to exclude from the area of medical concern the man whose drinking has not progressed to dependency. The great majority of alcoholics coming to hospital have however reached this stage.

INTRODUCTION TO TREATMENT

Three major reviews of the literature on treatment of alcohol dependence (see Hill and Blane, 1967) have largely served to show that claims for the efficacy of specific treatments and treatment regimes have outrun the evidence. Few investigators have attempted any sort of control, few authors have defined the characteristics of the population they are treating, few have given a full and clear description of the treatment employed, and few have reported outcome in interpretable terms or troubled to check the validity of the data. Reports of outcome are often limited to consideration of abstinence alone. Bruun showed very little difference in outcome between patients at special alcoholism clinics and those treated routinely. Strict and critical assessment of the literature forces the conclusion that the value of any of the wide range of specific treatment methods has still to be incontravertably demonstrated. What is effective may well be the rather non-specific influences of support, understanding, exhortation and education. A number of basic points will be considered below before going on to discuss specific treatments.

Natural history of alcoholic dependence

There is little evidence on what happens to untreated alcoholics; the background against which to judge the impact of modern treatment is largely lacking. Lemere tried to fill in the gap by collecting life histories of 500 deceased alcoholics who were relatives of his patients. He concluded that 28% of alcoholics would drink themselves to death, 7% would regain partial control, 3% would return to moderate drinking, 29% would continue to have a problem throughout their lives, 22% would stop during a terminal illness and 11% would stop, exclusive of a terminal illness; the average age at death was 52 years. Kendall and Staton followed up for a mean of 6.7 years 62 alcohol-dependent patients who had been assessed at the Maudsley but who had either refused treatment or been considered unsuitable for treatment. Comparison with a series of treated patients from the same hospital suggested that the results of therapeutic intervention were far from dramatic, and yet the report seems to indicate that treatment probably conferred some advantages. But it must be stressed that Kendall and Staton were not comparing matched groups, and no-one appears to have overcome the ethical difficulties involved in carrying out the obvious experiment of randomising patients between treatment and nontreatment control groups.

Realistic treatment aims

Alcohol dependence is often a chronic relapsing illness and a treatment centre which sees its credit simply in the percentage—(always the minority)—of patients abstinent for one or two years is not really employing a proper measure of the efficiency of its programme. The patients who show longterm abstinence are often those of sound personality and good social stability, who were in any case likely to achieve abstinence with minimal therapeutic interference; their decision to stop drinking may cause them to seek treatment, rather than the treatment being causally related to abstinence. In realistic terms the work of an alcoholism treatment service, unless it rejects its immediate failures, is largely the long-term care of people more or less frequently in difficulties. Although it is still usually stated that the alcohol-dependent person never returns to normal drinking realism now necessitates the acceptance of the finding that return to normal drinking is the outcome for 5% of patients, although it would be rash to offer this to the patient as the desired aim.

A number of American authors have made the point that abstinence in itself is not an adequate treatment goal, and Gerard and his coworkers (1966) have shown that 'good' outcome as measure by abstinence may correlate with improved family, social and work adjustments but that the relationships are certainly not one-to-one. The abstinent alcoholic may still be grossly disturbed. Whether the correction of the underlying personality problem is a realistic treatment goal in any but a very small minority of cases is doubtful and helping a damaged and handicapped individual to adjust better to his environment may often be the best, and the useful best, which can be achieved. If the patient becomes abstinent much seeming abnormality of personality may turn out to be the consequence not the cause of inebriety. Furthermore the possibility of considerable personality maturation without intensive psychotherapy once the patient stops must be borne in mind before prescribing energetic treatment.

Finding and persuading the patient
Identifying the patient is obviously the necessary first step to treatment. There is evidence that in general practice (Parr, 1957), industry (Hawker et al., 1967) and in general hospitals (Blane et al., 1963; Green, 1965) the majority of patients suffering from alcohol dependence escape attention. The reason why physicians miss the diagnosis is partly their expectation that all alcoholics conform to the stereotype of the derelict.

The argument is however often heard that there is little to be gained from trying to woo the patient into treatment—he will not accept treatment until he has hit rock bottom. Hoff has for instance written, 'Perhaps the only thing that will ever bring an alcoholic to effective therapy is to hit bottom and forcefully experience the hard reality that his life is unmanageable.' The idea that motivation is something which we must leave for suffering to generate in our patients, rather than its being something which it is our responsibility to build, has been challenged by Sterne and Pittman : 'The motivation concept, as frequently applied to alcoholics, serves as a convenient rationale for unwillingness to review and modify current policies and practices so as to encourage the alcoholic to seek treatment and stay with it'.

The problem of how to persuade alcoholics to seek treatment and stay with it has been investigated by a group in Boston who found that if patients were offered immediate help rather than a long wait for a routine appointment they tended to stay in treatment. Wedel has come to much the same conclusion but has demonstrated that staying longer in therapy is not necessarily equivalent to doing better.

The patient's denial of his problem is certainly often an obstacle to intensive psychotherapy, and Moore and Murphy studying 100 alcoholics who received intensive psychotherapy showed a significantly negative correlation between outcome and denial rated on a five-point scale. The form in which the initial interview is cast is probably important: head-on confrontation may sometimes be effective but it is perhaps more likely to increase the patient's defensiveness.

It may be helpful, after carefully constructing the history of the typical drinking day to work through equally careful questioning directed to all possible areas in which drinking may be causing damage. For instance rather than just asking the patient whether he has ever lost a job through drinking it may be useful to probe in detail as to whether he is late for work, extends his lunch hours, takes days off, has received warnings, gets others to cover up for him, asks for subs, is aware of declining efficiency, has caused or had accidents at work, has missed promotion. Similarly detailed enquiries should be made into the happiness of the marriage, relationship with the children, social life in general, and financial status. A patient may be much more able to admit to small problem after small problem rather than suddenly admit to what must to him be a very frightening and shaming diagnosis. As in the course of history-taking he reviews his total situation he gradually convinces himself of the extent and seriousness of his problem. He probably never before sat down and made this thorough inventory.

When the full history has been taken it is then probably useful to offer the patient some simple explanation of what is meant by alcohol dependence, offering him the self-image of someone who is suffering from illness rather than moral failing, giving him the opportunity to move from the bad role to the sick role and thus to surrender his denial and defences.

Providing a total service

Lack of rigidity in the treatment approach to alcohol dependence is essential. Treatment cannot be envisaged in terms of a fixed course of so many weeks, a sort of package deal. Different patients have different needs, and although the specialised inpatient psychotherapy unit as pioneered by Glatt (1959) at Warlingham Park Hospital has obviously been an enormously influential demonstration which has done much in Britain to arouse medical interest and to overcome pessimism the specialised inpatient unit is not the appropriate treatment for other than perhaps the minority of patients. Walton et al. (1966) favoured three to four weeks inpatient care rather than the two to three months advocated by Glatt. Some patients may find the group and milieu therapy practised in specialised units too threatening (McPhail, 1965), patients who discharge themselves from the unit may do well (Rathod et al., 1966), and the value of brief superficial therapeutic intervention has recently repeatedly been stressed.

A therapeutic service must be able to deal with a whole range of needs, and deal with them properly. Thus in some instances lengthy inpatient care or skilled outpatient psychotherapy may be the requirement, but the demand for immediate help from the new patient who presents as an emergency or the old patient who presents in relapse must be met and here the ready availability of 'drying out' beds is a necessity. For the socially disorganised skid-row alcoholic something too must be provided and for this type of patient the specialised rehabilitation hostel is of increasing importance.

There is such very insufficient evidence as yet on what treatments are the most valuable and on what treatment setting, inpatient or outpatient, is most appropriate for any patient that it seems best to adopt attitudes of empiricism and eclecticism, to accept that the essential practical politics of treatment are a willingness to keep trying.

ALCOHOL WITHDRAWAL

Here certainly is an aspect of the treatment of alcohol dependence where no rigid formulae can be applied. Not all patients require heavy medication or intensive medical care and yet for some patients withdrawal precipitates a potentially fatal syndrome which demands skilled nursing and very intensive medical treatment.

Judgement as to whether a patient should be admitted to hospital during the withdrawal period depends partly on the severity of his symptoms and whether he has had a previous history of delirium tremens or withdrawal fits. The decision must also be influenced by whether he has a family who can look after him, an interested A.A. sponsor who will visit him, and a general practitioner who can keep an eye on him at home. It seems likely that in these favourable circumstances outpatient withdrawal of alcohol is a feasibility, and indeed encouraging the patient to get off alcohol in his own home usefully rallies his support.

Mild or moderate withdrawal symptoms, whether dealt with on an outpatient or an inpatient basis, can be treated with any one of a variety of sedative and tranquillising drugs but symptoms in any case are apt to clear fairly quickly. Although drugs are useful the benefit they confer is probably often only marginal: chlordiazepoxide ('librium') has been widely used and on the whole the evidence is that it is effective, although there are conflicting results. Chlormethiazole ('heminevrin') also is of some use.

Treatment of delirium tremens is a very different matter, however, and Victor has suggested that a proper regime must include a thorough search for medical complications, good nursing care, correction of fluid and electrolyte loss and sometimes of hypoglycaemia, a careful watch on temperature and blood pressure, and immediate symptomatic treatment of hypothermia or circulatory collapse which can be sudden with fatal complications. Cutshall has emphasised how much may be achieved simply by good general nursing and medical care.

Victor also discussed drug use in delirium tremens, and this question is one which has attracted much debate. Victor as well as Jaffe are of the view that once the patient has actually developed the delirium the ability of any drug to cut short the illness is uncertain. Oral paraldehyde in doses of 10-12 ml. in orange juice is perhaps the drug of choice. It is not logical to use the phenothiazine derivatives, for they exhibit no cross-tolerance with alcohol, and Thomas and Freedman (1964) have shown superiority of paraldehyde over promazine.

Gessner has argued that if the treatment of delirium tremens can be regarded simply as treatment of withdrawal from a cerebral-depressant drug then the model of barbiturate withdrawal should be used and delirium tremens should be treated with alcohol; Thomas and Freedman (1965) argue against this proposal. High potency vitamin injections may be necessary for the correction of coexisting vitamin deficiency, but are not a specific treatment for delirium tremens. Routine treatment with phenobarbitone to prevent withdrawal fits is probably not necessary.

SPECIFIC TREATMENTS

Antabuse

'Antabuse' (disulfiram) has been in use for almost 20 years but evaluation is still surprisingly difficult. Patients who continue to take antabuse have a better prognosis than those who stop the drug but this obviously cannot be taken as a causal connection. Wallerstein appeared to demonstrate that antabuse gave results superior to aversion treatment, group hypnotherapy or milieu therapy but the methodology of that trial is open to criticism.

What has clearly emerged from the years of experience is that antabuse is not a drug without side effects. It can produce tiredness, depression, malaise, bad breath, gastrointestinal symptoms, urinary frequency, breathlessness, impotence, dermatitis, peripheral neuropathy and toxic confusional states while the antabuse-alcohol reaction can cause cardiac irregularities or even death. Antabuse should therefore only be given under proper medical supervision and as the drug, though slowly absorbed, is cumulative the dose may have gradually to be reduced. The usual maintenance dose is 0.25 to 0.5 g/day.

The argument for carrying out an antabuse-alcohol test reaction while the patient is in hospital is that unless he has actual experience of the consequences he may be tempted to experiment with drinking on top of antabuse when he leaves hospital, with consequent serious danger. The opposing argument is that even a controlled reaction in hospital is too dangerous to be justified, and that the patient is as much forewarned by verbal explanation as by the potentially fatal therapeutic experiment. If a test reaction is carried out the usual routine is to load the patient with 1 g. antabuse/day for five days and then give 2 oz. whisky with careful charting of pulse and blood pressure, and to institute immediate treatment with vasopressors, hydrocortisone, and antihistamines intravenously if shock should develop. The reaction results in acetaldehyde intoxication (due to block of alcohol breakdown) and histamine release.

Citrated calcium carbimide ('abstem')

This drug which is given in an oral dose of 50-100 mg./day, has an action somewhat like antabuse but is more rapidly excreted so that the patient can drink without symptoms within 24 hours of the last dose. The intensity of the reaction with alcohol is probably milder than the alcohol-antabuse reaction and the long-term side-effects less frequent. As the drug is quickly absorbed it is effective after a single dose.

Aversion therapy

Aversion treatment has been in use even longer than antabuse, but despite the enthusiasm of the early reports of emetine aversion, experiments with apomorphine, use of electric shock and succinyl apnoea as the unconditioned stimulus there is still uncertainty as to whether conditioning has anything to offer. Franks (1966) has reviewed the relevant literature at length and points out that physicians have seldom applied conditioning procedures with the attention to learning theory which is required if conditioned effects are indeed to be established.

Alcoholics Anonymous

Alcoholics Anonymous is a world-wide organisation but in particular countries it takes on particular characteristics. In England (Cooper and Maule, 1962) its membership is perhaps drawn rather more from the middle classes than from the unskilled, its emphasis is not particularly on religion, and the two-way relationship with the medical profession is excellent. Claims for percentage of success in treatment are difficult to assess but whatever the absolute figures there is no doubt that A.A. is operating as an enormously valuable supportive organisation. Only a minority of patients who are encouraged to join A.A. will in fact do so and the type of patient who will affiliate is so difficult to predict that the best course is to encourage every patient at least to go and see what A.A. has to offer. Williams has described a dining club for former alcoholics. In several cities Alanon family groups have been established to help the spouse of the alcoholic.

Group and special psychotherapies

Group therapy for alcoholism has in recent years been widely practised. Although comparison between series treated at different hospitals presents obvious difficulties (Glatt, 1967), it seems likely that equally good results can be obtained with individual treatment on a well-staffed general psychiatric ward as with group treatment on a specialised unit.

The percentage success rate possibly depends more on the general intensity of care than on whether group or individual methods are used, and Vallance (1965) has certainly shown that when alcohol-dependent patients are treated in a busy general mental hospital ward where staff are short of time results can be disappointing. Clancy et al. comparing two treatment methods showed that group therapy did not improve outcome while Gerard and Saenger (1966) showed that although outpatient group therapy did not improve results it was associated with better clinic attendance.

Hypnotherapy has been widely used in the treatment of alcohol dependence for about 80 years, but it can again only be noted that the evidence of efficacy is lacking. LSD has recently been widely used as an adjunct to psychotherapy in alcoholism, and although this approach may produce striking but transitory immediate changes in feeling and behaviour the balance of evidence to date is that LSD is not of much value. The use of psychodrama and of autogenic training has also been advocated. Lemere and O'Holleren employed thiopentone abreaction.

Other physical methods

Milligan claimed good results when alcohol-dependent patients were given ECT two or three times a day to the point of complete confusion, and Marconi et al. treated three patients by thermocoagulation of the dorsomedial nucleus of the thalamus. These reports are not easy to assess. Taylor has stated that metronidazole ('Flagyl') will remove craving for alcohol and also produce an antabuse-like reaction, but despite a number of favourable reports the evidence is unconvincing (Gelder and Edwards, 1968). The long term use of anti-depressant drugs or tranquillisers is ineffective.

Special Hostels

Myerson using a hospital ward as a night hostel showed that 54 out of 101 skid-row alcoholics who would probably have been considered by most experts as virtually untreatable could if given this sheltered base go out to work and maintain periods of sobriety. Only 12 patients were able to return to independent functioning and Myerson made the point that the majority of these destitute alcoholics required very long-term, or possibly life-time support, rather than any fixed 'course of treatment'.

Clearly a hostel is as well (or better) equipped to serve this long-stay function as is a hospital, and there has recently been in England a growing interest in the potentiality of the specialised alcoholism hostel. Not all these houses are concerned with the skid-row patient; an experiment has also taken place in setting up a hostel which functions as a therapeutic community and aims at intensive milieu therapy. Wilbur et al. (1966) show however the need for caution: skid row alcoholics submitted to the demands of a therapeutic community relapsed more quickly than patients in a control group, and it is necessary to stress that so far very little satisfactory work has been done to evaluate objectively the results which hostels can achieve.

Use of compulsion

In England the Mental Health Act is occasionally invoked to place in hospital a patient who has developed an alcoholic psychosis or who appears to be suicidal, but the general feeling seems to be that compulsion has no part to play in the long-term treatment of alcohol dependence. In America a number of experiments have been made on the use of probation and the supervised taking of antabuse by the chronic drunkenness offender, and some of the results appear to be promising (Ditman and Crawford, 1966). Mechanic has shown that if detained and voluntary patients are treated in the same institution the voluntary patients tend to do as badly as detained patients, rather than the voluntary influencing the detained for the better.

SUPPORTIVE PSYCHOTHERAPY

Whatever the lack of evidence in the literature clinical experience suggests that it would be altogether too destructive to conclude that no treatment ever helps the alcohol-dependent person. It would probably be nearer the mark to say that at times almost anything can be of help, provided the therapist is enthusiastic. This is a familiar statement in other areas of treatment, but to get beyond the vague assertion that offering a relationship is what matters and to dissect out and measure the effective elements within the encounter between physician and patient is a task which presents an enormously difficult challenge. Today the most important research probably lies in understanding processes of attitude change.

Below are some provisional guide lines for carrying out supportive psychotherapy with the alcohol-dependent patient: it must be stressed however that at present there is no research evidence to permit the assertion that this list is either complete or correct.

1. The therapist should be willing to show emotion, to give praise and encouragement, and sometimes to show anger.
2. Dependence on the therapist should at times be accepted.
3. The therapist should be willing when necessary to be directive.
4. Reality-help should be forthcoming.

5. Discussion is best centred on the here-and-now, and psycho-dynamic interpretations are seldom useful other than in terms of identification of patterns of behaviour.

6. If a patient fails to keep an appointment he should be contacted.

7. Treatment goals should be realistic for otherwise either patient or therapist will terminate treatment.

Such therapy may often be carried out as well by an experienced psychiatric social worker as by a doctor.

The PSW certainly has a very important part to play in working with the alcoholic's wife. Whether the disturbed behaviour of the spouse, which seems sometimes to be directed at forcing the patient back onto drink, is indeed directed by such pathological motivation, or whether alternatively it is merely the confused reaction of a largely normal person who has suffered much stress has been the subject of discussion. The value of supportive casework with the family has recently been shown by Evans et al (1966); a treatment team may be able to do much to alleviate the suffering of the family even if the patient cannot stop drinking.

SUMMARY GUIDE

Based on the interpretation of all the evidence which has been discussed above there is set out in this section a treatment scheme in summary form. Because the central conclusion from the foregoing review can only be that the best treatment for any particular patient is still often a matter of trial and error, and because what clearly emerges is that uncertainty much exceeds the certainties, it is only right to point out that this scheme is no more than provisional and personal.

1. *The initial interview*

(a) The diagnosis of dependence is established; this diagnosis implies total abstinence as the best treatment goal but reality dictates that this is often an ideal rather than a practicality. (b) An assessment is made of the patient's physical, mental, and social state and any immediate necessary measures instituted. (c) The meaning of the diagnosis and the purpose of treatment is fully and carefully discussed with the patient.

2. *Withdrawal*

(a) *Outpatient:* If the patient is not physiologically dependent and if he has good social support, withdrawal may be attempted on an outpatient basis. Chlordiazepoxide (10-20 mg. t.d.s. orally) is probably the drug of choice.

(b) *Inpatient:* (i) If the patient is severely physiologically dependent he must be admitted. Severity of dependence can however be difficult to assess and if uncertain one should play safe: if the patient is already exhibiting minor hallucinatory phenomena or otherwise appears to be on the verge of D.T.'s, if he has previously experienced D.T.s or withdrawal fits or if he is drinking crude spirits, admission is indicated. For delirium tremens oral paraldehyde (10-12 ml.) is probably the drug of choice.

(ii) If the patient lacks social support admission will more often be necessary.

(iii) Admission is mandatory if the patient is depressed. The risk of suicide must always be borne in mind.

(iv) Failure of outpatient withdrawal may be an indication for admission, but if a patient has been admitted several times in quick succession for drying out it may be best not to offer too easy readmission, but rather to suggest that (with help) he invests more effort.

3. *Setting up for psychiatric treatment*

(a) *Outpatient:* In the majority of cases it is reasonable to institute outpatient care pragmatically as the first approach. If it fails then inpatient care is indicated.

(b) *Hostel:* (i) Patients who have lost all social support may often be admitted direct to a hostel after withdrawal or, if the hostel has adequately skilled staff, for withdrawal. Preliminary hospitalisation is by no means always necessary.

(ii) The hostel may also be used as a half-way house for the patient who has received inpatient care but who is not yet ready for independent living.

(c) *Inpatient:* (i) In carefully selected cases admission to a specialised alcoholism treatment unit may be necessary: criteria for selection probably approximate to those for moderately intensive individual psychotherapy.

(ii) Admission may at times be useful simply to remove from stress and chaos the patient who is failing to maintain more than transient sobriety, and to provide a period in a controlled environment which will hopefully enable the patient to make a new start.

(iii) Admission may be indicated for further detailed assessment or treatment of concurrent psychiatric abnormality, for example for investigation of possible dementia, establishment of differential diagnosis between alcoholic hallucinosis and schizophrenia, treatment of depression or of sexual deviation.

4. *The content of treatment*

(a) Supportive psychotherapy and supportive casework with the family are the essence of treatment.

(b) Introduction to A.A. should usually be arranged.

(c) As regards specific treatments the only essential is to avoid exposing the patient to unnecessary danger or distress, and to avoid substituting other addictions for dependence on alcohol. With this proviso the treatment in which the therapist is most expert and most interested is the one to be preferred.

5. *Relapse*

Relapse in the majority of cases is to be expected and an important attribute of a truly effective treatment service is its ability to maintain contact with patient and family so that relapse can be dealt with speedily and before too much damage is done.

6. *The patient who fails to respond*

Sadly, despite every therapeutic effort there are patients who simply go on drinking. Nevertheless if the offer of help is kept open even in the seemingly most hopeless case the unexpected may eventually happen—and in the meantime much can be done to help the family.

REFERENCES

BLANE H. T., OVERTON W. F. and CHAFETZ M. E. (1963) *Quart. J. Stud. Alcohol*, **24**, 640.

BLUM E. M. (1966) *ibid.* **27**, 259.

COOPER J. and MAULE H. G. (1962) *Brit. J. Addict.* **58**, 45.

EVANS M., FINE E. W. and PHILLIPS W. P. (1966) *Brit. med. J. i.* 1531.

FRANKS C. M. (1966) *Int. J. Addict.* **1**, 61.

GELDER M. G. and EDWARDS G. (1968) *Brit. J. Psychiat*, **114**, 473.

GERARD D. L. and SAENGER G. (1966) *Outpatient Treatment of Alcoholism.* Brookside Monograph No. 4, University of Toronto Press, Toronto.

GLATT M. M. (1959) *Lancet*, ii, 397.

GLATT M. M. (1967) *ibid.* i, 791.

GREEN J. R. (1965) *Med. J. Aust.* i, 465.

HAWKER A., EDWARDS G. and HENSMAN C. (1967) *Med. Offr.* **117**, 313.

HILL M. J. and BLANE H. T. (1967) *Quart. J. Stud. Alcohol.* **28**, 76.

ISBELL H., FRASER H. F., WIKLER A., BELLEVILLE R. E. and EISENMAN A. J. (1955) *ibid.* **16**, 1.

JELLINEK E. M. (1960) *The Disease Concept of Alcoholism.* Hillhouse Press, New Brunswick.

KEPNER E. (1964) *Quart. J. Stud. Alcohol.* **25**, 279.

LORAND S. (1945) in *Yearbook of Psychoanalysis*, Vol. 1, International Universities Press, New York, p. 359.

MCPHAIL D. (1965) *Lancet*, ii, 75.

PARR D. (1957) *Brit J. Addict.* **54**, 25.

RATHOD M. H., GREGORY E., BLOWS D. and THOMAS G. H. (1966) *Brit. J. Psychiat.* **122**, 683.

THOMAS D. W. and FREEDMAN D. X. (1964) *J. Amer. med. Ass.* **188**, 316.

THOMAS D. W. and FREEMAN D. X. (1965) *ibid.* **193**, 78.

VALLANCE M. (1965) *Brit. J. Psychiat.* **111**, 348.

WALTON H. J., RITSON E. B. and KENNEDY R. I. (1966) *Brit. med. J.* ii, 1171.

WILBUR B. M., SALKIN D. and BIRNBAUM H. (1966) *Quart. J. Stud. Alcohol* **27**, 620.

WORLD HEALTH ORGANISATION (1964) *Technical Report Series*, No. 273 W.H.O., Geneva.

Behaviour Therapy

M. G. GELDER

Institute of Psychiatry,
Maudsley Hospital, London

Any discussion of the place of behaviour therapy among psychiatric treatments must start with a definition, for we soon encounter a problem which is familiar in psychiatry: the term has more than one meaning. For this reason arguments arise which are based on mutual misunderstanding rather than any fundamental divergence of opinion. On the one hand behaviour therapy describes a group of specific techniques of symptomatic treatment which are based directly on the results of experiments on learning carried out in the psychological laboratory. The techniques have been newly devised and owe their existence to these preliminary experimental studies. On the other hand some enthusiastic advocates of behaviour therapy use the term more widely to include in addition techniques of treatment which can be explained in retrospect in terms of observations and theories of learning but which originated in other ways. For example techniques of psychodrama, especially those which include role rehearsal, are included among the behaviour therapies by some authors, while Wolpe and Lazarus (1966) in the book 'Behaviour Therapy Techniques' discuss such methods as abreaction and Laverne's technique of carbon dioxide therapy.

Differences of this kind are crucial when results of behaviour therapy are considered, for two therapists may be describing the effects of quite different ranges of treatment techniques.

In this account the term behaviour therapy will be used in

the first way, that is to mean a group of techniques specifically based on learning principles. It will be seen that these techniques often have to be combined with other more traditional methods, including those of psychotherapy. When this is done we shall consider that the behaviour therapy has been combined with another method. We shall not adopt the practice of calling 'behaviour therapy' any treatment which a behaviour therapist finds both useful and at the same time understandable in terms of learning principles.

Before coming to specific techniques it is also important to realise that even some of those behaviour therapy methods which were developed directly from laboratory experiments about learning share many features with other treatments which have evolved in quite different ways. For example systematic desensitization, Wolpe's pioneering contribution to the behaviour therapies has many features in common with autogenic training a method little used in Britain but widely exploited on the European continent, and also with Kretschmer's fractionated active hypnosis. Equally, some of the methods used for tics and writer's cramp find parallels among the techniques devised by Leonhard and described in his book on individualized psychotherapy (1963). Of course the mere existence of these related methods does not detract from the importance of the behaviour therapies, but it does sound a warning against accepting too readily the proposition that the methods work because, and only because, of the learning processes on which they are supposedly based. Quite other therapeutic processes may be at work.

Careful experimental study is needed to establish a relation between learning processes and therapeutic outcome and there is already some evidence in desensitization that the learning may not take place exactly as originally supposed. As we shall see later, systematic desensitization treatment may act through processes of habituation rather than by reciprocal inhibition of anxiety, the principle on which it was first constructed.

However, although it will ultimately be necessary to know

the precise mechanisms at work in each treatment so that each can be refined and made more effective it is possible at this early stage in the life of behaviour therapy to proceed empirically, seeking to discover the value of each treatment before its mode of action is fully understood. There are in psychiatry, after all, a great many treatments of known worth whose precise mode of action is still uncertain: electroconvulsive therapy and the tricyclic antidepressant drugs provide everyday examples. Conversely, because a treatment is based on an impressive body of psychological experiments it need not necessarily be of practical value. Only careful clinical evaluation of each technique can decide its therapeutic potential.

In the account which follows a brief description will be given of the three most important techniques of behaviour therapy: systematic desensitization, aversion therapy, and operant conditioning. In each case we shall consider the present state of knowledge about the indications for treatment, the results obtained with suitable patients, any adverse effects which have been observed and the most probable mechanisms by which changes are brought about. As far as possible statements will only be made if there is supporting statistical evidence from clinical trials, although space does not allow all the evidence to be set out in detail here.

SYSTEMATIC DESENSITIZATION

(a) *The technique*

The patient is exposed to a graded series of situations which evoke anxiety and at the same time anxiety is counteracted in some way, usually by muscle relaxation but sometimes by hypnosis or by anxiolytic drugs such as the ultra-short acting intravenous barbiturate methohexitone sodium ('brietal') (Friedman 1966). The anxiety-evoking situations may be presented by asking the patient to imagine them—the most convenient and flexible method—or by asking him to undertake a series of graded tasks which expose him to the real objects of his fear. Each situation is presented repeatedly until it evokes no more anxiety before proceeding to the next.

A 'hierarchy' of stimuli can thus be dealt with one by one, starting with that which evokes minimal anxiety and progressing systematically to those which originally provoked most anxiety. As the patient is desensitized to each new stimulus so the anxiety-response to the next stimulus in the hierarchy is diminished by a process of stimulus generalization, and it in turn becomes amenable to desensitization. The technique of desensitization is easy to learn but considerable practice and skill are needed in constructing effective hierarchies from the tangled mass of fears which most patients present (see Wolpe and Lazarus 1966). It is worth spending much time with the patient in this stage of hierarchy construction, for on it depends much of the success of the treatment.

(b) *Indications*

Systematic desensitization produces its best results in the treatment of simple circumscribed phobias. Many controlled studies have been carried out with volunteers whose simple phobias have been great enough to limit certain aspects of their lives, but not sufficiently distressing to have made them seek psychiatric treatment on their own initiatve. These investigations amply confirm the value of the treatment in such disorders, and they have shown it to be significantly more effective than either no treatment, or other brief treatments, and also more effective than either relaxation or stimulus repetition carried out separately (Paul 1967, Rachman 1965).

Controlled investigations have also been carried out with subjects who had more intense, but still isolated, phobias which had caused sufficient distress to make them seek psychiatric treatment on their own initiative. Again the results of desensitization treatment are significantly better than those of supportive treatment, or of brief psychotherapy given either individually or in a group (Gelder, Marks and Wolff, 1967). Indeed it is with patients with such isolated phobias that the most striking effects of desensitization have been obtained, and it is proving to be the most useful brief treatment for many such cases.

Of course, such discrete phobias are uncommon—they account for only about 2% of the neurotic disorders seen at the Maudsley Hospital. The phobic patients seen most often in a psychiatric clinic are those with the syndrome of agoraphobia or with rather similar phobias of travelling. Desensitization produces less striking changes in these patients, and the results vary with the severity and complexity of the condition. Patients with very severe agoraphobia did not respond significantly better to desensitization than to a control treatment of brief re-educative psychotherapy (Gelder & Marks, 1966). However, patients with less severe agoraphobia responded better and after six months desensitization had improved significantly more than a matched group of patients receiving individual or group psychotherapy (Gelder, Marks and Wolff, 1967). Certain characteristics of the more severe phobic cases are particularly important in predicting the outcome of desensitization.

Thus the more widespread the neurotic symptoms other than phobias, the more severe the associated obsessional symptoms and the greater the general (or free floating) anxiety the poorer the response to desensitization. Marked interpersonal problems are also associated with poor response. Correspondingly it has been found that when these problems are first dealt with by psychotherapy a response to subsequent desensitization is faster, even though the phobias do not change during the initial period of psychotherapy (Gelder and Marks, 1968). Lazarus reported a similar finding with volunteer subjects.

When patients with agoraphobia are treated by desensitization other methods of treatment often have to be combined, in contrast to the specific phobias where desensitization is usually enough. Some discussion of interpersonal relations is especially important, and so are social measures with the family. Lazarus refers to this combination of treatments as 'broad spectrum behaviour therapy', but it seems better to regard it as a combination of the new behavioural technique of desensitization with the established methods of psychotherapy and social work.

Other conditions than phobias can be treated with desensitization, provided anxiety or its somatic equivalent is evoked by clearcut environmental stimuli. Certain psychosomatic disorders fall into this group, including asthma (Moore 1965) nervous diarrhoea, and some patients with anorexia nervosa in whom a food phobia is prominent (Hallsten, 1965). Some sexual disorders can also be treated, notably frigidity (Brady, 1966), and certain cases of impotence (Wolpe, 1958). In both, treatment is directed to the patient's fears about heterosexual relationships. Some homosexual patients in whom similar fears are prominent can also be treated in this way, but there are no controlled studies on which to judge the value of the method.

Syndromes which respond badly to desensitization include obsessional neuroses and writer's cramp.

(c) *Changes during treatment*

The initial changes which occur in suitable patients are quite specific. There is some evidence that immediately after a desensitization session both anxiety and phobias are reduced significantly, while other symptoms including depression change very little. Over the next week, general anxiety gradually returns to its original level but phobias, though they relapse in part, do not regain their former strength. When the next session starts a week later some of the improvement in phobias is retained to be added to the improvement in the new session—and so improvement builds up from week to week. In one investigation (Gelder and Marks 1968) it was shown that of the symptoms rated, it was only the phobias which changed in this progressive way.

However, further improvement does occur more indirectly,

being gradually built on the core of improvement in the phobias or other desensitized symptoms. Relieved of some of this burden phobias patients become more outgoing and improve both in their work adjustment and in their interpersonal relations. Follow up studies have shown that a group of patients with simple phobias or milder degrees of agoraphobia had not relapsed significantly when rated three years after treatment began.

(d) *Adverse effects*

Two kinds of adverse affects might follow desensitization treatment: symptom substitution and social repercussions. Symptom substitution is expected, on the basis of psychodynamic theories of neurosis, whenever symptoms are treated directly. The problem is more complex than it first appears, because it is not sufficient to show that when one symptom is treated by desensitization another appears. Neuroses often run a fluctuating course and new symptoms come and go over the years. To prove symptom substitution it must be shown that the new symptom was not present at times before treatment, and the findings must be compared with those in a control group of similar patients. There is a further difficulty: it is necessary to take account not only of specific symptoms but also of social adjustment. Patients sometimes avoid symptoms at the expense of limiting their lives. When these problems have been taken into account no definite evidence of symptom substitution has been found after desensitization.

The social repercussions of behaviour therapy were described by Crisp in an uncontrolled study. He described the appearance of problems in other members of the family as the patient improved. Such occurrences are familiar to psychiatrists and can arise whenever the patient rather than the whole family is the focus of treatment. However, there is again no controlled evidence to indicate that the problem is met more often after desensitization than after other kinds of psychotherapy directed to the individual.

(e) *Mechanisms of treatment*

Does desensitization really act through deconditioning mechanisms, or does it produce changes in some other less specific way? The treatment could for example, easily act as a powerful medium of suggestion. However comparisons of desensitization with direct hypnotic suggestion have shown that desensitization has a greater effect on phobias than does suggestion, at least when volunteers with simple phobias are studied. When the two treatments are compared in patients with agoraphobia the difference is less because the specific desensitization component becomes progressively impaired as levels of general anxiety rise and the suggestive components play a correspondingly greater part.

Is it the complete desensitization procedure which is effective: i.e. is it necessary to combine relaxation and stimulus repetition or would either alone be enough? There is now considerable evidence that the complete procedure is needed: relaxation alone is less effective than the whole method as is graded re-exposure without relaxation. (Kondas 1967; Lomont and Edwards 1967; Rachman 1965).

The effect of the doctor-patient relationship has been shown to be insufficient to account for the results of desensitization both by comparing desensitization with interviews lasting an equivalent length of time and by arranging tape recorded desensitization sessions in which the therapist is absent.

The question remains whether desensitization really acts by reciprocal inhibition of anxiety as Wolpe suggested. He supposed that the anxiety evoked by each imagined stimulus is counteracted by super-imposing an anxiety-reducing agent (usually relaxation) and that this in turn leads to deconditioning. An alternative suggestion has been put forward by Lader and Mathews on the basis of psychophysiological experiments reported by Lader and Wing (1966). These authors have demonstrated that the response to repeated arousing stimuli varies according to the patient's level of anxiety. When this is low repetition leads to habituation, i.e. each new stimulus produces less arousal than the one before. If, however, anxiety is very high repetition fails to produce habituation and may even result in progressively increasing responses. Lader and Mathews suggest that the function of relaxation in desensitization is to reduce general anxiety to a level at which repetition of stimuli leads to habituation. In words this suggests that the psychological mechanism at work is habituation rather than reciprocal inhibition. Some evidence for this was obtained by Lader, Gelder and Marks (1967) who found a significant positive correlation between the rate of habituation measured in the laboratory and the clinical outcome of desensitization treatment.

AVERSION THERAPY

(a) The technique

The technique of aversion therapy for alcoholism using emetine or apomorphine as the aversive stimulus is too well known to require further description. More recently the technique has been modified and its indications have been widened to include other conditions, notably certain sexual disorders.

The change in technique has been to use mild electric shock as the aversive stimulus instead of emetine and apomophine. This makes the treatment much less unpleasant, both for patients and staff, than the older method with its repeated induction of vomiting. The faradic shocks need not be strong for they can be timed precisely—an important consideration as effective conditioning depends on precise time relations—and can be repeated many times without the habituation which often occurs when apomorphine and emetine are used repeatedly.

The usual method is to attach electrodes to the forearm or leg and to give mild shocks from a battery powered shock-box. The method is safe and the patient is asked to regulate the strength of the shocks to a level which neutralizes any pleasure he feels in the situation but does not produce intense pain. These shocks can then be associated repeatedly with the deviant behaviour in two ways.

It can be carried out in reality: a transvestist may be asked to dress in women's clothes and shocked whenever the clothes are on, but allowed to escape from shocks by taking them off quickly. Alternatively the behaviour can be imagined and shocks given when the patient signals that he has a clear mental image. Imaginary stimuli have the advantage that they allow behaviours to be treated which cannot be carried out in the clinic e.g. homosexual patterns of behaviour. Also by dealing with the patient's fantasy life they treat a vital early stage in the chain of behaviour which starts in fantasy and leads to overt behaviour.

A number of variations in the technique have been described which incorporate different schedules of reinforcement. There is good experimental support for the use of partial reinforcement at some stage of treatment, but it is still uncertain whether better results follow other modifications such as the method of anticipatory avoidance training described by Feldman and McCulloch (1965).

(b) *Indications for Aversion Therapy*

Pharmacological methods of aversion therapy began with the treatment of alcoholism but are now seldom used in this condition because controlled investigation failed to show any advantage over simpler methods using group therapy and disulfiram ('antabuse') (Wallerstein 1957). More recently McCance has reported a controlled investigation of faradic aversion therapy for alcoholism and again no advantage was found over a more traditional treatment regime.

Faradic aversion therapy has been used in a number of sexual disorders. As yet there are no fully controlled comparative trials of aversion therapy and other treatments in these conditions. The statements which follow are therefore based on less secure evidence than those which were made about desensitization treatment.

The best results to date have been obtained in patients with transvestism and fetishism. Of a group of 12 treated at the Maudsley Hospital 11 (90%) improved at the end of 2 weeks' twice-daily treatment and about 8 (66%) were still judged improved a year later. Preliminary results indicate that trans-sexual patients respond less well. Although 4 out of 5 in our series improved at the end of treatment only one was rated improved a year later. Of a group of 18 homosexuals and paedophiliacs about 70% had responded by the end of treatment while 50% (of the 10 so far followed for 1 year) were still judged improved a year later. Feldman and McCulloch (1965) report comparable results with homosexuals: 58% were rated improved a year after treatment. In the absence of control groups of patients treated in other ways these findings are hard to assess, for case selection may possibly have biased them and in any case little is known about the natural history of their conditions. However, they are certainly encouraging enough to demand further investigation.

Of course aversion treatment can only suppress deviant be-haviour; heterosexual behaviour will develop only if it was present to some extent before treatment and can be encouraged afterwards. Bancroft's findings with homosexuals are particu-larly instructive. Ratings were made of the level of homosexual and heterosexual behaviour at five periods in the patient's life: in adolescence, at five years and two years before treatment, and at one and two years after treatment. These ratings showed that the effect of treatment was to restore the patient's sexual adjustment to about the level which had obtained in adolescence. They were, so to speak, given a fresh start and what happened in the year after treatment was of prime importance. Aversion therefore needs to be followed by measures to encourage better heterosexual adjustment no matter which sexual disorder is treated. These measures may take the form of desensitization of the social anxieties which have prevented the patient enjoying female company; or counselling, or some form of psychotherapy to deal with more deep-rooted interpersonal difficulties or sexual anxieties; or marital counselling to help restore healthy relations between the patient and his wife.

Aversion therapy has also been tried in problem gamblers (Goorney 1968) in obesity (Meyer and Crisp 1964) and in addiction to cigarette smoking (Franks 1966). It is still too early to evaluate the results, but the methods deserve further investigation.

Amongst transvestists, the group of patients which does best, further criteria for selection are being identified. The fewer associated neurotic symptoms, the better the result; aggressive and psychopathic personality traits are probably unfavourable, and so is the absence of any ability to take part in heterosexual relations. Of course these finer indications may be picking out patients who have a good long-term prognosis even without treatment of any kind, but even if this is so the changes after aversion therapy are very much more rapid and certain than could be expected by chance. In other words aversion may be markedly accelerating the natural processess of recovery.

(c) *Adverse effects*

When aversion therapy was first used in sexual disorders fears were expressed that it might provoke worse difficulties, including psychoses. Careful follow up has not so far shown any evidence of this. Temporary emotional reactions to treatment have been noted, but these can be dealt with promptly (Marks and Gelder 1967). Many patients show transient depression during treatment and in some this may outlast the treatment, especially in those who have had previous depressive illness. The repeated shocks which have to be given may give rise to aggressive feelings at some stages of treatment but these can be dealt with if they are recognised promptly and discussed, and have not outlasted treatment in our patients.

Aversion therapy leads to alterations at several levels of psychological function. Sexual arousal to the deviant stimuli is inhibited, but because the inhibition is highly specific it does not lead to any general sexual impotence. At the same time attitudes to the objects of the sexual deviation change in a specific way so that no unfavourable attitudes develop towards normal sexual relationships.

Lastly, there is a gradual loss of the pleasure previously associated with deviant sexual fantasies and in about half the patients we have treated a gradual suppression of these fantasies. Thus patients could no longer imagine deviant fantasies deliberately, nor did they experience them spontaneously after treatment except transiently. This suppression, which appears to be a form of internal avoidance response, presumably explains why so few patients experience direct conditioned anxiety. It is unusual for patients to report after treatment that the sight of their fetish objects provokes anxiety. Instead they describe a lack of feeling.

Systematic investigation has shown also that the changes depend on the use of shocks (Marks and Gelder 1967). Repetition of stimuli without shocks produced very much smaller changes in the functions measured during treatment.

(d) *Ethical considerations*

Aversion therapy raises ethical problems which are not met in desensitization. The treatment uses punishment in the technical psychological sense: i.e. it uses stimuli which reduce the probability of occurrence of the response with which they are linked. However many of the conditions treated with aversion therapy are among those which society punishes in the judicial sense. It is most important that the aversion therapy plays no part in punishment in the judicial sense and can be seen by all to be separate from this. Thus the patient must want treatment himself. Of course most patient's motives are mixed and it may be difficult to assess motivation, but a careful evaluation must be made.

Fortunately the treatment demands the close co-operation of the patient and cannot work without it. This is a valuable safeguard: aversion therapy cannot brainwash an unwilling patient. It is also usually better not to carry out aversion therapy as part of treatment demanded by a court e.g. as a condition of probation, and if this is done it must be made absolutely certain that the treatment plan accords with the patient's own wishes. However, if these precautions are taken aversion therapy can be carried out quite ethically.

OPERANT CONDITIONING

These methods are based on Skinnerian operant conditioning, which stresses the powerful effect which rewards have when they are made contingent upon the subject's own behaviour. Desired patterns of behaviour are met by immediate reinforcement, and a procedure called shaping allows behaviour patterns to be drawn out and elaborated from small beginings.

Operant conditioning is therefore mainly useful as a means of building up new behaviour patterns, or restoring those which have been lost in the course of illness. In animals and in normal children, using food as a reward, the techniques have been shown to be capable of producing rapid and effective learning. However in adults, and particularly in psychiatric patients, there are practical difficulties because effective rewards are often hard to find; the problems are similar to those of finding incentives in a rehabilitation programme. For very regressed schizophrenic patients food can sometimes act as a reward; in others tokens have been used which can be exchanged for goods or for extra privileges on the ward. Social reinforcements i.e. praise from another person whom the patient respects, is the most natural reinforcement but some patients (e.g. chronic withdrawn schizophrenics) have difficulties in making relationships, and this may preclude social rewards, at least in the early stages of treatment.

The indications for this form of treatment have not yet been worked out clearly and there are no satisfactory controlled studies which would enable its value to be judged relative to better established methods of treatment and rehabilitation. A large number of reports exist, many of which are of single cases, and these show that it is possible to use the methods in a variety of disorders. These include behaviour disorders in normal and retarded children (Bijou 1965, Bijou and Orlando 1961) mutism and other behavioural disorders of chronic schizophrenia (Ayllon and Haughton 1962) and of infantile autism (Ferster and de Meyer 1961; Risly and Wolf 1967; Wetzel et al. 1960), tics (Barrett 1962) and stuttering (Flanagan et al. 1958; Goldiamond 1965).

Patients may be treated singly or whole wards of patients may be treated together as in the so called token-economy wards. In these, nurses are instructed to ignore abnormal behaviour but to reward desirable behaviour promptly. Tokens are used as rewards and patients have to earn tokens in order to gain privileges such as cigarettes, the use of a billiard room, or a weekend pass. The programme must be carefully adjusted to the needs of each patient on the ward so that no one is set an impossible task and yet each has a set of clearly defined goals to work towards. The reported results of such token-economies have been striking, but they have been instituted in back wards and it is not yet certain whether the results are better than those of more conventional programmes of social rehabilitation carried out with equal drive and enthusiasm.

SELECTION OF PATIENTS FOR BEHAVIOUR THERAPY

From what has gone before it will be seen that the skills which are required in choosing patients for behaviour therapy are the traditional skills of the psychiatrist rather than any body of specialized psychological knowledge. Psychological expertise comes later when treatment begins and the details of the deconditioning process are worked out.

There are several stages in case selection. It must first be decided whether any kind of symptomatic treatment is appropriate.

This requires a careful psychiatric evaluation of the patient and his relationship with other members of the family. It must be decided how far the presenting symptoms are the real focus of his difficulties and how far they are really protecting the patient from other anxieties or problems in his family or in his life outside. If careful evaluation suggests that symptomatic treatment is likely to be helpful the next stage is to decide whether behaviour therapy can be expected to offer this effectively. This depends on knowledge of the detailed indications which are being established for each technique of behaviour therapy, but all the indications depend on clinical phenomena which the psychiatrist is well used to assessing.

First, certain syndromes are more amenable to treatment than others: desensitization is most useful for simple phobic states, rather less so for agoraphobias; it is valuable in certain psychosomatic disorders with a marked situational element; much less useful in obsessional states and of no proven value in hysteria. Among the sexual disorders aversion therapy is probably most effective for transvestism and fetishism, less so for homosexuality, least effective for transsexual patients. This kind of information about syndromes is gradually being added to all the time.

Indications can be refined further by looking more closely at the individual symptoms which make up the syndrome, and at the personality. For example within the syndrome of agoraphobia the presence of marked obsessional symptoms or a high level of generalized anxiety indicate poorer response to desensitization. With transvestism the presence of many associated neurotic symptoms indicates a poor prognosis. Personality must also be taken into account, and again clinical assessment is at present just as valuable as the use of specialized psychological measurements. Thus patients with marked problems in interpersonal relations and severe emotional difficulties have been shown to respond less well to desensitization. Among homosexuals those with hysterical personalities traits do well (Feldman and McCulloch 1965). These observations can be linked with the preceding ones in that emotional difficulties are the main source of the generalised anxiety which has already been shown to be associated with poor response to treatment.

Finally, especially in choosing patients for desensitization, the assets of the patient's personality have to be weighed to decide what use he will make of any symptom relief which behaviour therapy affords him. Similarly aversion therapy merely damps down deviant sexual impulses; some heterosexual interests must be developed later, and this also needs a certain maturity of personality.

This list of indications will no doubt have given rise to a mounting conviction that patients who do well with behaviour therapy are those who would have a good prognosis with any treatment, or for that matter, with no treatment at all. Our comparative studies of desensitization confirm this assertion in one respect but qualify it significantly in another. Most of the indications of good response of phobics to desensitization are also indication of good response to psychotherapy; the one exception is that high anxiety levels are relatively more important in desensitization. However desensitization produces more *speedy* recovery of phobias than does psychotherapy given to comparable patients. Similarly, though it is possible that many of the transvestists and homosexuals who respond to aversion therapy would be expected to do well, given enough time, whatever treatment they receive they improve very much more rapidly with aversion therapy. We can therefore think of behaviour therapy as a treatment which speeds up natural processes of recovery. Since natural recovery presumably depends in many cases on fortuitous relearning experiences it is not surprising that the carefully organised learning experiences in behaviour therapy are more rapid and effective,

The question of the value of behaviour therapy then becomes one of a time-budget: how much faster will recovery follow this treatment than another treatment or no treatment at all? And how long a course of behaviour therapy is needed to achieve this?

If two weeks' treatment of a transvestist can bring about changes which would otherwise take a few years, then it may reasonably be said to be useful. So also if desensitization for a few months of weekly outpatient treatment can bring forward recovery which would otherwise take many years. In other words we have to consider not only the final effectiveness of treatment as measured in, say, a followup at 5 years; we have also to consider the cost-effectiveness of treatment as measured by the length of treatment and length of time which spontaneous recovery would reasonably have been expected to take.

Thus careful study of behaviour therapy techniques can provide not only a series of powerful new treatments for selected patients, but also necessarily leads to further investigation of the long-term course of patients with neuroses and sexual disorders. In this way behaviour therapies are generally coming to occupy an important place in psychiatry.

REFERENCES

AYLLON T. and HAUGHTON E. (1962) Control of the behaviour of schizophrenic patients by food. *J. Exp. anal. Behav.* **5**, 343-352.

BARRETT B. H. (1962) Reduction in the rate of multiple tics by free-operant conditioning methods. *J. Nerv. Ment. Dis.* **135**, 187-195.

BIJOU S. W. (1965) Experimental studies of child behaviour normal and deviant. In *Research in Behaviour Modification*. Ed: Krasner, L. and Ullman, L. P. New York, Holt Rhinehart and Wilson

BIJOU S. W. and ORLANDO R. (1961) Rapid development of multiple schedule performances with retarded children. *J. Exp. anal. Behav.* **4**, 7-16.

BRADY J. P. (1966) Brevital-relaxation treatment of frigidity. *Behav. Res. and Therapy*, **4**, 71-77.

FELDMAN M. P. and McCULLOCH M. J. (1965) The application of anticipatory avoidance learning to the treatment of homosexuality: I. Theory technique and preliminary results. *Behav. Res. and Therapy* **2**, 165-183.

FERSTER C. B. and DeMEYER M. K. (1961) The development of performance in autistic children in an automatically controlled environment. *J. Chronic. Dis.* **13**, 312-345.

FLANAGAN B., GOLDIAMOND I. and AZRIN N. H. (1958) Operant stuttering: the control of stuttering behaviour through response contingent consequences. *J. Exp. anal. Behav.* **1**, 173-177.

FRANKS C. M. (1966) An improved apparatus for the aversive conditioning of cigarette smokers. *Behav. Res. and Therapy*, **4**, 301-308.

FRIEDMAN D. E. (1966) A new technique for systematic desensitization of phobic patients. *Behav. Res., amd Therapy*. **4**, 139-140.

GELDER M. G. and MARKS I. M. (1966) Severe agoraphobia: A controlled prospective trial of behaviour therapy. *Brit. J. Psychiat*. **112**, 309-319.

GELDER M. G. and MARKS I. M. (1968) Desensitisation and phobias: a cross-over study *Brit. J. Psychiat*. **114**, 323-328.

GELDER M. G., MARKS I. M. and WOLFF H. H. (1967) Desensitisation and psychotherapy in phobic states. A controlled enquiry. *Brit. J. Psychidt*., **113**, 53-73.

GOLDIAMOND I. (1965) Stuttering and fluency as manipulatable operant response classes. In *Research in Behaviour Modification*. Ed. Krasner, L. and Ullman, L. P. New York, Holt, Rhinehart and Wilson.

GOORNEY A. B. (1968) Treatment of a compulsive race gambler by aversion therapy. *Brit. J. Psychiat*., **114**, 329-334.

HALLSTEN E. A. (1966) Adolescent anorexia nervosa treated by desensitisation *Behav. Res. and Therapy*, **3**, 87-91.

KONDAS O. (1967) Reduction of examination anxiety and 'stage fright' by group desensitisation and relaxation *Behav. Res. and Therapy*, **5**, 275-281.

LADER M. H., GELDER M. G. and MARKS I. M. (1967) Palmar skin conductance measures as predictors of response to desensitisation. *J. Psychosom. Res*. **11**, 283-290.

LADER M. H. and WING L. (1966) Physiological measures, sedative drugs, and morbid anxiety *Maudsley Monograph No. 14*. Oxford University Press.

LEONHARD K. (1963) *Individualtherapie der neurosen*. Jena. Gustav Fischer Verlag.

LOMONT J. F. and EDWARDS J. E. (1976) The role of relaxation in systematic desensitisation *Behav. Res. and Therapy*. **6**, 11-25.

MARKS I. M. and GELDER M. G. (1967) Transvestism and fetishism: clinical and psychological chages during faradic aversion *Brit. J. Psychiat*., **113**, 711-729.

MARKS I. M., GELDER M. G. and EDWARDS G. (1968) Hypnosis and desensitisation for phobias; a controlled prospective trial *Brit. J. Psychiat*. In Press.

MEYER V. and CRISP A. H. (1964) Aversion therapy in two cases of obesity. *Behav. Res. and Therapy*, **2**, 143-147.

MOORE N. (1965) Behaviour therapy and bronchial asthma: a controlled study *J. Psychosom. res*. **9**, 257-274.

PAUL G. L. (1967) Insight vs. desensitisation in psychotherapy two years after termination *J. Consult. Psychol*. **31**, 333-348.

RACHMAN S. (1965) Studies in desensitisation: I. The separate effects of relaxation and desensitisation *Behav. Res. and Therapy*, **3**, 245-251.

RISLEY T. and WOLFF M. (1967) Establishing functional speech in echolalic children *Behav. Res. and Therapy*. **5**, 73-88.

WALLERSTIEN R. S. (Ed.) 1957 *The Hospital Treatment of Alcoholism.* London Imago Press.

WETZEL R. S., BALER J., RONEY M. and MARTIN M. (1966) Outpatient treatment of autistic behaviour. *Behav. Res. and Therapy*, **4**, 169-177.

WOLPE J. (1958) *Psychotherapy by Reciprocal Inhibition.* Stanford University Press.

WOLPE J. and LAZARUS A. A. (1966) *Behaviour Therapy Techniques.* Oxford Pergamon Press.

Notes on Anxiety

ANDREW SODDY

St. John's Hospital,
Stone, Aylesbury

There is no precise clinical definition of anxiety. It is a feeling that everybody recognises because everyone has felt it. It consists of a subjective impression associated with restlessness and autonomic symptoms which can be objectively studied. At best it is a normal emotion with a biological value, at worst a pathological symptom that can exert crippling influence on a person's life.

Denis Leigh at the World Psychiatric Association's Symposium in London in November 1967 described anxiety as a 'universal human experience, a normal concomitant of living in a world that threatens existence, and in which struggle against the environment, both internal and external, is part of Man's lot.' Lader at the same meeting said that 'there is no definition of anxiety more satisfactory than the simple human statement 'I am anxious.' I think that this sort of unhelpful generalisation is a reflection of the present unsatisfactory state of ideas about anxiety.

The diagnostic fashions with regard to anxiety are also confusing. Anxiety is said to be a component of many depressive states to the extent that they have been called anxiety neuroses. On the other hand in the past ten years this has gone out of fashion and many people now would regard all cases presenting with anxiety as cases of concealed depression. Prior to 1905 the word does not appear as a technical term in English textbooks. Freud did not talk about anxiety but about fear and *angst*. This German word is difficult to translate into English but means something much wider than anxiety. The psychiatric distinction between anxiety and fear consists in the presence and reality of the thing apprehended (Lewis). Anderson describes anxiety as objectless fear. However there is a good deal of overlap between the terms anxiety, fear and phobia.

INHERITANCE AND ENVIRONMENT

Like many other features of personality anxiety is a characteristic which tends to run in families. Starting with a genetically diverse population of rats and pairing the most and the least emotionally reactive individuals with their own litter mates it is possible to breed out separate strains which are increasingly dissimilar in emotional make-up. Tested by their fear response (the number of pellets defaecated on exposure to mild stress such as an unfamiliar bright and noisy open area) these strains of rats showed further divergence in each generation, suggesting that many different genes contributed to the inheritance of behavioural traits.

Human studies on the inheritance of neurosis have been based mainly on three types of investigation. Firstly, physiological, using individuals for the study of autonomic response and twins for comparative work. Secondly, personality questionnaires for self-rating of emotional instability or neuroticism. This is used almost exclusively amongst twins. Thirdly, clinical studies of the frequency of neurotic illness among relatives of patients.

The physiological investigations have been concerned with response to stimuli; heart beat frequency and breathing rate following a sudden noise or flash are typical examples. When pairs of monozygotic and dizygotic twins were tested in an attempt to minimise all but genetic differences the role of the genetic make-up was confirmed, in that the responses of monozygotic twins were found to be significantly more alike although by no means identical.

Personality questionnaires have seldom set out to measure anxiety specifically. Of the commonly used questionnaires (M.M.P.I. and Cattell's High School Personality Questionnaires) significant intrapair differences between monozygotic and dizygotic twins have been found for such factors as general neuroticism and psychasthenia (fears and phobias). Inconclusive results have been obtained on a number of other assessment scales. However, Shields has shown strong evidence for a genetic predisposition to neurosis in studies of monozygotic twins reared apart. In twin studies of this sort differences between monozygotic and dizygotic groups rest on moderate correlations between monozygotic pairs and low correlations between dizygotic pairs.

In the clinical studies the difficulties include the problem of exact diagnosis, comparability between different workers, the drawing of an arbitary line between normal and abnormal, and contamination (members of a family appear to suffer from the same neurosis; with the possibility that being familiar with one another's symptoms they give a misleading impression of their own condition). Recent studies have taken precautions against contamination (for example, blind diagnosis of each individual case).

The investigation of families of anxiety neurotics suggests a figure of 15% incidence of similar conditions in close relatives. Cohen and co-workers found 55% for the frequency of anxiety neurosis in mothers of chronic male patients with the same condition. Coppen and his group reported that the only high correlation in respect of neuroticism was between male patients and their mothers. Sheild's work with monozygotic and dizygotic twin pairs shows the contrast to be greater for the type of condition than for the presence or absence of psychological disorder in general.

The most recent study be Shields and Slater included an uninterrupted series of same sex twins, monozygotic and dizygotic, one member of each pair being treated at the Maudsley between

1948 and 1958. This series seemed to represent a fair sample of the general population since no excess of twins was referred and the ratio of monozygotic to dizygotic was normal. Of seventeen monozygotic probands with anxiety state 47% had twins with some psychiatric disorder. Of twenty-eight dizygotic probands the corresponding figure was 18%. But if the criterion is the same diagnosis the concordance rate for monozygotic twins fell to 41%, for dizygotic to 4%. These findings strongly suggest a degree of genetic specificity for anxiety. Interestingly, when both members of a pair of twins had anxiety states there were often considerable differences in their actual symptoms.

Thus the evidence available confirms that inherited factors play a part in predisposition to anxiety but twin studies show that the effect is hardly overwhelming and the influence of the environment may often be predominant. Nobody of course believes that neurosis could be purely hereditary. But argument rages between environmentalists and interactionists, between those who hold that the events of post-natal life alone decide the neurosis, and those who believe that inherited constitution and life experience together work for a neurotic outcome.

One of the first people to make a significant contribution to study of the action of environment was Freud. In general he began by thinking of anxiety as a by-product of sexual frust-ration, and finally noted that it was related to the loss of someone who was loved and longed for. Anxiety was the reaction to the danger of loss, and the pain of mourning was a reaction to the actual loss of the object. Thus pathological anxiety arises from disturbances in the relationship a person has with some other being and is quite distinct from real danger. In Freud's view some anxiety is inescapable and he recognised the neuro-physiological and biochemical basis of anxiety.

More recently Bowlby has postulated that pathological anxiety often arises from situations which lead to frequent alarm during period of prolonged isolation from attachment figures. He says that later studies have confirmed the correctness of Freud's views and have shown that the behaviour accompanying fear and that accompanying anxiety are of two diametrically opposed sorts. For fear elicits escape behaviour and anxiety attachment behaviour.

Separation anxiety is clearly seen in children with an unsettled home life in their early years. A longitudinal study by Moore in 1967 showed that anxiety in later childhood was associated with two kinds of early experiences; placement in daily care with someone other than the mother and placement in care with a number of persons. After the third birthday children were not affected by such conditions. Studies on monkeys confirm that young primates if separated from a mother figure later show exaggerated separation anxiety.

Bowlby believes that recent work on the role of affectional bonds in birds and animals may hold the clue to the reasons why a human being should experience anxiety on separation. In mammals the first and most persistent bond is between mother and the young, but there are others and it is characteristic of mammals that bonded pairs stay together. Should they be separated each will seek the other out and renew proximity. Attempts to separate them are strenuously resisted and on separation they become agitated and distressed showing all the signs of separation anxiety. These bonds can be independent of food and sex and it seems that they develop because young creatures are born with a bias to approach sources of certain classes of stimuli and to avoid others. Experience tends to make the animal readier to approach familiar stimuli and avoid unfamiliar ones. Thus the familiarity of the mother strengthens the bond. Later in life other attachment figures appear and attachment behaviour towards them serves the purpose of protection from predators. Separation anxiety develops whenever behaviour is thwarted or seems likely to be thwarted.

In amplifying Bowlby's views Parkes has described studies of bereaved human adults. The behaviour patterns associated with the urge to recover a lost object are crying, searching and angry protest. These are useful activities, for crying and searching help the separated parties find each other while protest punishes all concerned with the loss and makes it less likely to occur. Parkes' studies show that after the death of a person to whom they are attached the bereaved tend to call and search for the lost one. The awareness that the search is useless causes the searcher to avoid, deny and restrict the expression of his search. When a person searches for a dead loved object not only is there restless movement but there is a perceptual and ideational component to the search. All but two of the twenty-two widows he interviewed said that they felt restless and fidgety during the first month of bereavement, the motor activity being directed towards finding the lost person, though as the searcher rarely admits to this aim the activity is categorised as aimless. Hyperactivity lasts a year or more but declines. It is associated with preoccupation with thoughts of the dead person and with a clear visual image of him. Half the widows said also that they felt drawn towards places or objects associated with the dead husband. Several had turned over the idea of suicide in their minds, thinking to join the dead person after death. Crying for the lost object is also a common feature of the search. In children such a search may be responsible for some fugues.

An aspect of anxiety which is usually overlooked in Britain has been described by von Baeyer of Heidelberg. He has dealt specifically with anxiety as a phenomenon bound to a political and social situation governed by terror. He showed that the conscious, situation-adapted, fear of real dangers could be converted after the real danger had passed to free floating anxiety with fear experiences reproduced in dreams.

He followed up survivors of such terror from pre-World War II Germany and found that over one third had significantly lasting psychiatric effects of their experiences. It was common to find that the fear produced by the situation of persecution had given place to a lasting anxiety state deeply rooted and irreversible by therapy. A further 40% of his follow up were disturbed by phobias and nightmares. He had no control group, but others have demonstrated a much higher incidence of anxiety than is found in non-persecuted populations. The persistence of anxiety did not appear to be related to ethnic characters or to the reasons for persecution or to loss of family, or even to social adjustment afterwards. These states persisted in people who were well adjusted before the episode and in people of all ages.

This development from fear to anxiety is explained by modern experimental psychology in terms of learning theory: anxiety is a conditioned response to fear. The primary drive is pain. Neutral stimuli associated with pain cause fear responses and the consequence of these responses is a secondary drive stimulus of anxiety. Another neurological approach emphasises the brain structures involved. Thus the anterior parasympathetic part of the hypothalamus seems to be connected with aggression mechanisms, the smaller posterior sympathetic part with fear and adversive reactions. The hypothalamus in turn is controlled by the limbic system including the amygdala and hippocampus. Part of the amygdala controls fear reactions and part aggression. The hippocampal effect on fear reactions opposes the amygdalic one. Thus the amygdala and hippocampus appear to constitute a control mechanism.

The reticular formation is also thought to be concerned with the fear reaction, stimulation causing cerebral arousal increasing with stronger stimuli to panic and fear. Its influence may override that of other centres. Some of these brain areas can be affected by psychotropic drugs.

TREATMENT OF ANXIETY

There are several different ways of treating anxiety and obviously a knowledge of the aetiology of the anxiety in a particular patient may indicate the treatment most likely to succeed. The treatment alternatives are drug therapy, milieu therapy, psychotherapy, surgery, and techniques such as desensitization (see 'Behaviour Therapy', p. 41).

In *milieu therapy* Sivadon (Paris) treats anxiety by progressive adaptation between the anxious patient and his fears, but does not restrict this to a single technique like desensitization. He believes that the symptoms of anxiety are a function of the immediate environment and he therefore adjusts the whole social milieu so that the patient gradually comes to accept situations previously intolerable to him. This differs from desensitization in that it involves careful and continuously supervised management that can only be done as an inpatient. This does not mean that all anxiety-producing factors are removed or that total support is given—this would be self-defeating in the end—but a careful manipulation of both. Thus moderate stress in a supportive environment is held to be therapeutic.

In the therapeutic milieu active participation in small groups encourages social integration. Simple things such as the right-sized room (high spacious rooms increase anxiety), the arrangement of furniture, and seating arrangements round a table can all influence anxiety. Active involvement in a common task for example meals, workshop tasks, and plays is a powerful factor in social integration. The basic pattern of therapy which Sivadon describes is rhythmic alternation. After an initial period of settling down patients are exposed to contrasting situations. The interplay of frustrating and supportive influences prepares the patient for return to the real world.

The introduction of *brain surgery* thirty years ago by Moniz for the relief of intractible and crippling symptoms created a 'psycho-surgical stampede' with indiscriminate operating on all kinds of chronic psychotic patients. The results can be seen in the long stay wards of all mental hospitals and since then there has been an inevitable reaction against such widespread use. However, frontal lobe operations have been found to give good results in anxiety and obsessional states, and in severe affective disorders (depression and anxiety tension). This is still important for dealing with selected patients resistive to other therapies. Lewin (1961) considers that rostral leucotomy yields good results for anxiety and depression and cingulectomy for aggression and obsessional disorders.

In everyday practice, however, most anxious patients are likely to be treated with drugs, and here for anxiety and tension barbiturates have still to be bettered despite numerous claims to the contrary. Their drawback is that they are liable to cause addiction (withdrawal then results in more anxiety, tension etc.), and the suicide problem is greater. Some patients do undoubtedly respond better to chlordiazepoxide ('librium') or meprobamate ('equanil') than to barbiturates although it is difficult to tell beforehand who will. It is important always to bear in mind individual variation and to be flexible in choice of drug and choice of dosage to achieve good results.

In emergencies with acute anxiety amylobarbitone sodium ('sodium amytal') 400-600 mgm. orally, sometimes with chlorpromazine, 100 mgm. orally, will prove successful. The chlorpromazine can be given intramuscularly if necessary, and so of course can the barbiturate. It is better, however, to avoid using a phenothiazine (chlorpromazine) if possible, since it may blur features of the clinical picture necessary for considered diagnosis, and for chronic anxiety phenothiazines are usually rather ineffective.

The chronic states, particularly in those who have always reacted to minor stress with excessive anxiety, can be well treated with phenobarbitone 30 mgm. t.d.s. or more, or with amylobarbitone ('amytal') 45 mgm. t.d.s. 'Drinamyl' (dextro-amphetamine 5 mgm. plus amylobarbitone 32 mgm.) is a useful drug for some inadequate personalities, for relieving anxiety due to the inability to cope with everyday tensions, particularly when some depression is present, but must be used with caution because of the risk of addiction. It should probably not be given for very long periods, and certainly not without frequent review until its effects in the particular patient are well established.

Increase in restlessness and anxiety are signs to change the drug, not to increase the dose from the recommended one tablet twice or thrice daily.

Where a non-barbiturate sedative is wanted, perhaps to ring the changes a little, meprobamate ('equanil', 'miltown', etc.) can be used in doses of 400-800 mgm. t.d.s. It carries risks of drowsiness, addiction, suicidal use like a barbiturate, and is more expensive. More popular just now, and probably better, are the diazepines—chlordiazepoxide ('librium'), diazepam ('valium'), oxazepam ('serenid D') and nitrazepam ('mogadon'). They are so new that there has not been time to gather wide experience of their possible drawbacks, such as the incidence of dependence. However, they seem safer than barbiturates in overdosage, and so may be better for the potentially suicidal patient. In customary doses for anxiety they also seem less liable to produce marked drowsiness. These are the lower ends of the dose ranges given below:

chlordiazepoxide	10-30 mgm. t.d.s.
diazepam	5-20 mgm. t.d.s.
	(10 mgm. i.v. for status epilepticus)
oxazepam	15-30 mgm. t.d.s.
nitrazepam	5-10 mgm. at night.

Finally a word must be said about the monoamine oxidase inhibitors phenelzine ('nardil', dose 15 mgm. t.d.s.) and tranylcypromine ('parnate', dose 10 gmg. b.d.), claimed by Sargant and his colleagues to be effective in phobic anxiety states of very long duration (up to twenty years) providing the patient's fears are free floating and diffuse, not fixed in a rigid pattern. The drugs may have to be continued for one to five years if relapse is not to follow withdrawal. Another condition for success is that the patient's previous personality should have been adequate, and according to Sargant the majority of patients with anxiety and tension states once had an adequate personality.

It may be that the success of the monoamine oxidase inhibitor drugs in the treatment of phobic anxiety states is an indication that these states are in fact related to agitated depressions. The relation between anxiety and depression and the proper sphere of these drugs is still a matter for research.

It must be remembered that the drugs carry a number of risks. Phenelzine may cause serious liver damage and marked hypotension, tranylcypromine may lead to a dangerous hypertensive crisis. In combination with other drugs or certain tryamine-containing foods hyperthermia, coma, and death may result. Contra-indicated drugs are narcotics (morphine, pethidine, etc.), analgesics, barbiturates and anti-depressant drugs such as amphetamine and the tricyclic compounds, sympathomimetic drugs and pressor agents. Foods contra-indicated are cheese, 'Bovril', 'Marmite', broad beans, alcohol, and coffee.

Specific treatment in depression

D. C. WATT

St. John's Hospital,
Stone, Aylesbury.

The depressive syndrome may occur in a variety of psychiatric settings, as a single clinical picture or in combination with other psychiatric or physical illness. This article discusses its specific treatment however it shows itself, provided it is sufficiently severe for the patient to be referred to a psychiatrist. The mild manifestations of depression, which recent surveys have shown are treated frequently by general practitioners, will not be considered nor will there be discussion of general psychotherapeutic and social measures which I nevertheless believe are mandatory accompaniments of specific treatment (see Shepherd et al., 1966).

Diagnosis resting upon a full case history is the indispensable basis for reasonable treatment and it is imprudent to curtail the time this requires by yielding to the importunity of the patient's urgings or distress. Sometimes complete enquiry will nevertheless yield possible alternative diagnoses and one then chooses the more probable or the one which more readily should yield to a particular treatment. One frequently neglected source of help in making a diagnosis is the course of previous attacks. About half the patients admitted to hospital with acute depressive illness have experienced attacks of such illness before. The completeness of recovery between attacks often distinguishes affective disorders from other conditions less amenable to treatment.

The earliest decision required of the psychiatrist concerns

71

admission to hospital. Where there is doubt my rule-of-thumb is to admit if illness prevents the patient from carrying out his usual occupation.

Specific anti-depressant treatment involves a choice between E.C.T. and tablets. E.C.T. gives the chance of quicker recovery but is more disturbing to the patient's life and work. For out-patients I frequently explain and leave the choice to them, allowing time for consideration and discussion with the family doctor or relatives. For in-patients the aim of treatment passes from preventing an interruption of work to restoration of working life as soon as possible. I therefore choose E.C.T. as the more rapid and effective remedy. Once again the psychiatric history gives valuable guidance; whatever specific treatment has pre-viously succeeded or failed is likely to succeed or fail this time.

The purposes of specific treatment must be clarified to decide the amount and duration of the specific employed. The primary aim is to terminate the attack as quickly, comfortably and safely as possible. A drug employed for this purpose should therefore be given in concentrated dosage for a limited time. I am most familiar with imipramine ('tofranil') and aim to raise an initial dose of 75 mg. a day over a period of 1 to 2 weeks to 300 mg. a day. I give an explanation of the side-effects to be anticipated to the patient, to his relative and to the family doctor. I advise modification of the dose for a temporary period when orthostatic hypotension is troublesome and adjustment otherwise to the maximum dose at which other side-effects are tolerable. Side-effects are often not important. Of 30 depressive in-patients rated for side-effects and treated with 300 mgm. desipramine ('pertofran') daily at St. John's Hospital, about one-third showed marked side-effects of which mouth dryness was the most prom-inent, but none required modification of dosage because of this. I continue drug treatment for four weeks but abandon it then if a substantial improvement has not occurred.

I prescribe other tricyclic compounds on the same principles. I believe it has been demonstrated (M.R.C., 1965) that monoamine oxidase inhibitors have no therapeutic action in depression of the degree discussed here and therefore I do not use them. This is particularly so in view of the dangerous side-effects which make dietary precautions necessary.

I usually prescribe E.C.T. twice per week and give ten treatments before abandoning it if a noticeable change has not taken place.

Two further facts about the outcome of depressive illness have an important bearing on the conduct of treatment; the frequency of subsequent attacks, and the frequency of chronic illness as an outcome. Lundquist showed on a thirty year follow-up that about 40% of recovered depressives had a further attack within 20 years, in close agreement with similar follow-up studies.* He also found that 20% of those in their first depressive attacks did not recover spontaneously in this time. In the M.R.C. trial of anti-depressive drugs 19% of all patients in the trial were undischarged at the end of six months.

We must therefore anticipate that $\frac{1}{5}$ of depressives will become chronic and half of the remaining $\frac{4}{5}$ who recover will have further attacks. A second aim of specific treatment therefore must be to establish a clear record of each treatment, given singly and adequately, and the patient's response to it. If the response is good this record will be the most valuable guidance available for treatment of future attacks; if it is poor the same treatment will not be given again unnecessarily through doubts about the adequacy of previous trial or uncertainty about its effect.

The obfuscation produced by combined treatments is a disservice to the patient: neither a successful nor adverse effect can be attributed to a particular drug and the fruits of previous experience are thus squandered.

Patients who do not recover on a thorough trial of one treatment may do so on another. In the M.R.C. trial of anti-depressant treatment, of 29 patients who did not respond to E.C.T. and a further 29 who did not respond to imipramine, 11 and 20 res-

*Of 380 patients with affective disorders admitted during 1967 to St. John's Hospital, 167 or 44% had had previous attacks.

pectively responded to an alternative treatment. Here again concurrent administration of more than one specific treatment, a change of treatment before a complete course is administered, or incomplete recording of the effect needlessly add ignorance and uncertainty to the hazards of future illness.

Chronic depressive illness takes the form either of continuous disability or of remissions so short as to produce substantial disability. The majority of patients suffering from prolonged depressive illness do ultimately recover. Until this occurs they need support and the preservation of the structure of their lives with judicious, spaced, thorough trials of the radical or palliative remedies available. Restraint in the use of sedatives and tranquillisers is especially needed in this vulnerable group to prevent dependence, overdosage and disabling intoxication. However, large doses of imipramine assist the recovery of some chronic patients. In St. John's hospital eight patients who had suffered from depressive illness for more than a year and had failed to respond to E.C.T., were given imipramine daily for a month, for half this time receiving 300 mg.-600 mg. daily, the effects being compared in a crossover trial with placebo. Five patients recovered with imipramine sufficiently to be discharged. Very few chronic patients will be so disabled as to require prolonged administration of an anti-depressant drug or E.C.T., but its occasional necessity is illustrated by the following case history.

Case 1. A married women in her thirties became depressed during the birth of her third child in 1956. It was not severe and she recovered, but two years later she became low-spirited, easily fatigued and irritable. Following a laparotomy in June of the same year she had a deep vein thrombosis and pulmonary collapse. During this illness she became deeply depressed and has never wholly recovered since. She was first admitted to hospital in September, 1958, and subsequently on 10 further occasions. In the six years after her first admission she spent 46 months in hospital.

Two admissions were preceded by suicidal attempts; her last admission was for 3 weeks in 1966.

She had several courses of E.C.T. and full doses of all types of anti-depressive drugs. She had imipramine 600 mg. daily and improved but became severely depressed when given less than 450 mg. daily. On this dose she subsequently had a severe leucopenia with intercurrent infection. Relapse occurred whenever these treatments were stopped and sometimes during their administration. In 1960 she had a leucotomy with temporary improvement.

She had E.C.T. every three weeks from May, 1965, having had it more frequently in the previous year. Under this regime she required sedative to sleep, was thin and had a poor appetite. She was listless but smiled in interview. She was able to do some housework, including cooking and shopping. She could feel herself relapsing at the end of each three-week interval between E.C.T. treatments. Throughout her illness she has received sustained support from her husband and general practitioner.

Leucotomy must be accounted a last resort for patients who have suffered and been disabled severely over several years without response to any other treatment.

Patients who have short remissions between attacks may be helped by prompt application of a specific treatment when an attack recurs. The following case-history illustrates a satisfactory application of this method:

Case 2. A married woman of 42, complained to her doctor early in 1962 of depression. He thought she might have been depressed for some months previously and that her symptoms were exacerbated by premenstrual tension. He prescribed 75 mg. imipramine daily and she was initially relieved, but symptoms recurred whenever the drug was stopped. Later she became worse and early in 1963 she was seen by a psychiatrist.

He found that her family and personal history were normal. She had two children and although her life was busy and she was conscientious no adverse circumstances were outstanding. She had had several spells of depression in 1962.

Her attack began with waking at 2 a.m. Her appetite was poor and she lost weight. She was low-spirited, worrying and irritable. She avoided social contact and felt conspicuous. She lost pleasure in things she usually enjoyed, lacked energy and had to make a special effort to carry out ordinary duties.

Imipramine was increased to 225 mg. daily and she recovered in ten days. About two months later she had another attack, for which 225 mg. imipramine daily was prescribed. The attack lasted 7 days.

Both the patient and her husband were medically trained and it was arranged that she would herself begin to take imipramine immediately should she have a further attack. She had an attack five weeks later, in the April, for which she started imipramine at once and which lasted three days. She had similar short mild attacks in August and October of that year (1963), treated in the same way. In November she had the most severe attack she experienced. She took 225 mg. imipramine daily and it lasted for 12 days. In February of the following year she had a mild attack which lasted 7 days.

No further attacks occurred up to the last contact with this patient four years later in March 1968. She had had at least 7 attacks in the 2 years preceeding this clear period. She had been continuously ill for seven months, with exacerbations, before seeing the psychiatrist, but the longest attack thereafter lasted 12 days.

Arranging the re-application of the treatment by the patient herself in this way requires a detailed knowledge of the course of the attacks and of the response to the drug. The earliest indications of the onset of an attack must be recognisable and unequivocal. The usual duration and degree of disability must be known and the time taken for treatment to produce a noticeable effect. An alternative to the prompt self-administration of imipramine arranged for this patient is to arrange for E.C.T. as soon as the patient notices the onset of illness. It is of course essential to have an articulate self-observant patient with attacks which are clearly recognisable in onset and termination and respond well to treatment, for such an arrangement to be effective. Prolonged continuous administration of imipramine had been advocated in Case 2 in the hope of preventing her attacks. I advised against it in this woman but there are perhaps cases who would gain from it. On the other hand must be reckoned the possibility of serious toxic reactions and the diminished feeling of well-being experienced by many patients while they are having the drug. A time comes when attacks no longer occur in many patients whose remissions are short, and the hope of this occurrence may reasonably be offered to them.

Sedatives are not a specific anti-depressive treatment but are frequently used to reduce the discomfort of the illness and to encourage sleep. I do not believe that insomnia is harmful, although it is a miserable experience, or that inducing sleep with sedative shortens a depressive attack. I regard night sedation simply as a comfort to the patient and a means of diminishing the disturbance at night. The disadvantage of hangover, which is frequent, and drug dependence which is less frequent, must be set against these gains. As with anti-depressive drugs therefore a sufficient dose of a single hypnotic drug should be given for a limited time. Night sedative should be stopped for a week before the patient's discharge. Outside hospital there is less control over what the patient takes, and stopping drugs before discharge lessens the risks of drug tolerance and dependence. Sedatives and minor tranquillisers administered during the day offer slight comfort to the depressive patient compared with the crippling possibility of habituation and dependence. They should therefore be reserved for severe agitation and also used briefly.

REFERENCES

SHEPHERD M., COOPER B., BROWN A. C. and KALTON G. (1966) *Psychiatric Illness in General Practice*. Oxford University Press, London.

LUNDQUIST G. (1945) Prognosis and course in manic-depressive psychoses. *Acta Psychiatrica et Neurologica*, Supplement 35. Stockholm.

MEDICAL RESEARCH COUNCIL (1965) Report by its Clinical Committee: Clinical trial of the treatment of Depressive Illness. *Brit. Med. J.*, I, 881.

Biochemical aspects of anti-depressants

D. M. SHAW

Neuropsychiatric Research Unit (M.R.C.),
Carshalton

Because the biochemistry of psychotropic drugs covers a large field the subject matter of this essay will be confined to reserpine, the tricyclic antidepressants, monoamine oxidase inhibitors, lithium and the use of certain amino-acids. All these substances share the common property that they may influence the metabolism of monoamines and may exert their therapeutic role by this means. This aspect of their functions has been stressed here but other explanations for their actions could prove to be of equal or greater significance in the future. Present concentration of attention on monoamines should not give a (spurious) sense of finality to what is still incomplete knowledge.

AMINES AND PATHWAYS

Monoamines are relatively simple organic substances containing one amine group ($-NH_2$). Some are very active biologically and the ones that concern us here come into this category. They are 5-hydroxytryptamine (5HT, serotonin), which is derived from the dietary amino-acid tryptophan, and noradrenaline which is synthesized from the dietary amino-acid tyrosine. Note that another dietary amino-acid, phenylalanine, is converted to tyrosine in the liver, and that an intermediate in the conversion from tyrosine to noradrenaline is dopamine, also a biologically active monoamine.

Both noradrenaline and 5-hydroxytryptamine are found in the central nervous system where they occur in the highest concentrations in the hypothalamus. High concentrations of 5-hydroxytryptamine are found in the limbic system as a whole. Dopamine is present in the caudate and lentiform nuclei, but adrenaline in contradistinction to noradrenaline appears to fulfil no role in the central nervous system. Noradrenaline, dopamine, and adrenaline are sometimes known collectively as catecholamines.

These high concentrations of amine are not present throughout the whole of the neurones but only in the terminal endings of the 'amine-utilizing' cells whose cell bodies lie elsewhere. Most of the noradrenaline and 5-hydroxytryptamine utilizing neurones have their cell bodies in the brain stem and most of the dopamine utilizing neurones lie in the substantia nigra. This term, amine-utilizing, has been chosen carefully to avoid entering the controversy whether amines act as transmitter substances at synapses or whether they function as modulators of neuronal function in another way. It is sufficient to say that noradrenaline and 5-hydroxytryptamine play an important functional role in the parts of the brain (hypothalamus, etc.) which are concerned with the mental and viscerosomatic manifestations of emotion.

The pathways by which amines are synthesized and degraded are simple and a cursory knowledge of them is necessary for a full understanding of current theories and the new work appearing in this field.

In the case of noradrenaline (and dopamine) (Fig. 1) the precursor substance tyrosine is hydroxylated to form the amino acid 3,4-dihydroxyphenylalanine (dopa). This step is catalysed by the enzyme tryosine 3-hydroxylase and it is the rate-limiting process in the formation of noradrenaline. Dopa is then decarboxylated to the monoamine, dopamine. If dopamine is to be further metabolized it is hydroxylated by dopamine β-hydroxylase to noradrenaline.

Noradrenaline is degraded down one of two pathways. In one the enzyme controlling the initial step is the mitochondrial

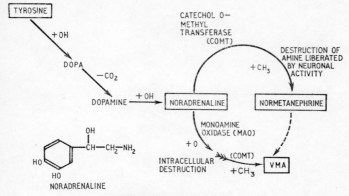

FIG. 1. Noradrenaline pathways.

enzyme, monoamine oxidase (MAO). The amine group is removed leaving an inert intermediary compound which is then methylated to vanillyl mandelic acid (VMA). The enzyme concerned in this second step is catechol O-methyl transferase (COMT). In the alternative route of degradation the initial step is O-methylation by COMT to form normetanephrine. Some of this is further degraded to VMA by MAO. However normetanephrine is the main product excreted in the urine when noradrenaline is metabolized initially by COMT, just as VMA is the main product in the urine from the first degradative route via monoamine oxidase.

The pathway for 5-hydroxytryptamine is very simple (Fig. 2). The precursor amino acid is hydroxylated to 5-hydroxytryptophan, and this in turn is decarboxylated to the amine, 5-hydroxytryptamine. The amine is destroyed by removal of the amine group by monoamine oxidase, and the final product is 5-hydroxyindolacetic acid.

We can now consider the amines in the context of a simplified model of an 'amine-utilizing' neurone (Fig. 3). This is only a

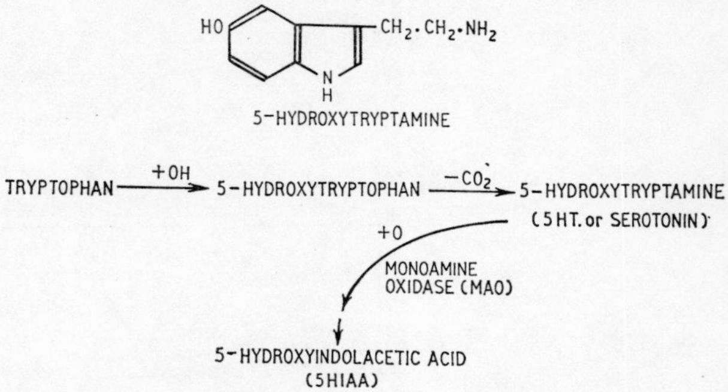

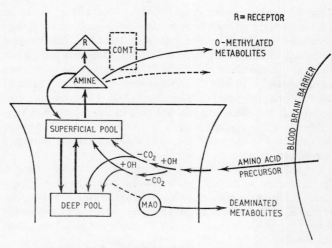

FIG. 2. 5-hydroxytryptamine pathways.

FIG. 3. Composite model diagram of 'amine-utilizing' neurone

model, a composite model which is based firstly on the behaviour of a number of tissues and secondly mainly on the behaviour of catecholamines. However, it probably represents what is going on in the neurones and it is probably valid for 5-hydroxytryptamine as well as for noradrenaline. The lower structure represents the distal (terminal) end pointing upwards of an 'amine-utilizing' neurone and above it, shown as part of a smaller rectangle, is the cell body of the next neurone in the pathway, with its receptor zone R and enzyme COMT. Both are separated from the plasma by the blood-brain barrier, and precursor amino-acids have to cross this to reach the surface membrane of the cell. The two amino-acids tyrosine and tryptophan share with other neutral amino-acids a common transport mechanism at the blood-brain barrier, but the amounts transported into the brain would not be a critical factor in the formation of amines unless an enormous excess of one amino-acid were present in the plasma. This might happen if large amounts of one amino-acid were ingested or failed to be normally metabolized as in phenylketonuria or other disorders of amino-acid metabolism, when such an excess could crowd other neutral amino-acids from the transport sites.

Let us suppose that tyrosine has crossed the blood-brain barrier and has gained access to the cell. The first stage, the rate-limiting step in the formation of noradrenaline is the conversion of tyrosine to dopa, and dopa is then decarboxylated to dopamine. It is not known exactly where these two steps occur in the cell but the final stage, hydroxylation of dopamine to form noradrenaline, probably occurs near the site of amine storage.

Noradrenaline is taken into one of two stores where it is inert, a loosely bound or superficial store and a larger deep store. Probably the superficial store is replenished by the deep store and the two are in equilibrium. In response to a nervous stimulus noradrenaline is released from the superficial store into the synaptic cleft, where it acts on the receptor site on the post-synaptic membrane.

Most of the free amine is inactivated by reabsorption across the pre-synaptic membrane. This is an active and highly efficient process which works against a considerable concentration gradient. However it is a two-step process, reuptake across the membrane and then rebinding in the stores, so that the actual concentration gradient presented to the reabsorption mechanism at the cell membrane is not as great as it seems. Any amine which escapes the reuptake mechanism either diffuses away extracellularly or is converted to O-methylated metabolites by COMT in the synaptic cleft.

Monoamine oxidase deals with any *intracellular* amine which is not rebound after reuptake or which escapes from the stores. The enzyme converts the amine to inactive deaminated products which are then lost from the cell.

Thus noradrenaline which is released by neuronal activity may appear in the urine as O-methylated products whereas that which is degraded within the cell appears as deaminated metabolites. This has been used as a means of gaining understanding of the actions of psychotropic drugs in a number of experiments.

The whole process is probably similar for 5-hydroxytryptamine except that there is no enzyme corresponding to COMT and any amine which escapes the reuptake mechanism working across the presynaptic membrane diffuses away.

We do not know exactly how the final levels of amine in the various pools are determined. It must be a complex equilibrium between synthesis, destruction, storage, leakage from the stores, physiological release, and negative feed-back mechanisms. There is negative feed-back between the end product of synthesis (the amine) and the enzyme which is rate-limiting in synthesis. As the concentration of amine rises so the tyrosine 3-hydroxylase or tryptophan hydroxylase is inhibited, thus reducing the rate of production of more amine. This is not the only controlling mechanism because it is nevertheless quite easy to alter the total concentration of brain amines by a variety of biochemical manipulations.

Besides being present in the brain MAO and COMT are found in other tissues in particular the gut, kidney and liver. They assist in the detoxication of potentially harmful amines.

SOME DRUGS

Reserpine

Reserpine is not a widely used psychotropic drug but it is included here because it has contributed a lot to our knowledge of the amines, it has been used extensively for the assessment of antidepressant agents, it is potentially dangerous when combined in certain ways with other drugs, and because it can produce psychotic depression in susceptible individuals. Of hypertensive individuals treated with reserpine a remarkably constant proportion of 12-15% develop psychotic depression as a complication of their treatment. The illness once established is not always dependent on the continuance of the drug, but the depression may persist and then seems to be similar to depression in patients whose illness was not drug-induced.

In animals reserpine and compounds with similar properties such as tetrabenazine produce a quite characteristic picture. They become inactive and do not respond readily to stimuli. This state has been termed 'reserpine-induced depression' and as such it has been used as an analogue of psychotic depression in man. It is true that antidepressant drugs frequently reverse 'reserpine-induced depression' in animals but it is not known to what extent the state produced by reserpine in animals is really comparable to the psychotic illness in man. It may be that there is no exact paradigm of severe depressive illness in the animal kingdom.

In the neuronal model reserpine acts somewhere on the pathway leading to uptake and storage of amine in the deep pool. When storage of amine in the deep pool is prevented the amine present or newly produced leaks away and is largely degraded by oxidative deamination. The superficial pool is in equilibrium with the deep pool so that much of the amine in the superficial pool is also lost. The overall picture is of a progressive and severe loss of cerebral amines. When reserpine is discontinued there is no instantaneous recovery. Eventually however the amine losses are reversed and their concentrations return to normal, although 5-HT and noradrenaline may recover at different rates. By the use of reserpine and other compounds differential depletion can therefore be produced at certain points in time. Numerous attempts have been made to evaluate the relative importance of noradrenaline and 5-hydroxytryptamine for behavioural recovery in animals using the times when one amine is depleted relative to the other. Unfortunately different results have been obtained not only in different species but also for different measures of behavioural recovery in the same species. It may be that under these abnormal conditions the gross concentrations of amine found in the brain give inaccurate indications of the amine available for physiological release at the synapses.

Chronically reserpinized animals eventually show some behavioural recovery from the inert unreactive state, presumably because of partial replenishment of the superficial pool by newly synthesized amine.

Tricyclic antidepressants

Imipramine is one of a group of tricyclic drugs which have antidepressant qualities, and as with our knowledge of amine metabolism much but not all of what we know comes from studies outside the central nervous system. It is interesting to see the close relationship structurally of the imipramine group to the phenothiazines (Fig. 4).

Imipramine has no influence on the two enzymes concerned with the destruction of monoamines, MAO and COMT. The brain content of 5-hydroxytryptamine, noradrenaline, and dopamine is virtually unchanged by the drug, but it will reverse reserpine-induced depression in animals. It appears to act on

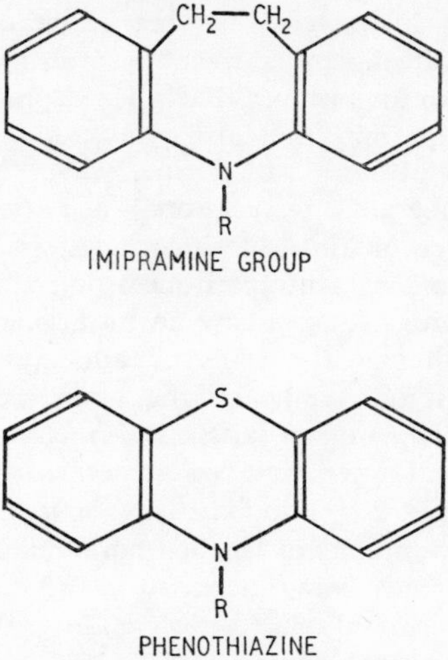

IMIPRAMINE GROUP

PHENOTHIAZINE

FIG. 4. Imipramine group and phenothiazine structures.

the processes which return amine into the cell endings after it has been liberated into the synaptic cleft. Imipramine and its related compounds inhibit or limit this process. Since reuptake is largely prevented the amount of amine present in the synaptic cleft after neuronal activity is increased and more is available to act on the receptors.

In the catecholamine hypothesis for depression it is suggested that this illness is due to a deficiency of noradrenaline in the brain. The antidepressant actions of imipramine are in line with this hypothesis, particularly as for a long time it was believed that imipramine influenced the reuptake of one amine only, noradrenaline. More recently it has been found that imipramine probably alters the tissue uptake of 5-hydroxytryptamine as well, so the antidepressant qualities of this drug no longer support the catecholamine hypothesis in its simplest form.

Nevertheless a lot of work has been done on the effects of imipramine on catecholamine metabolism in man and animals. It has been shown for instance that when depressed patients are treated with imipramine the urinary excretion of VMA goes down and that of normetanephrine, which is derived from noradrenaline liberated by neuronal activity, rises. Similar findings have been obtained by direct analysis of the brains of animals who received intraperitoneal injections of tricyclic antidepressant drugs followed by an intracisternal injection of radioactive noradrenaline. The tricyclic antidepressants decreased the uptake of noradrenaline by the brain tissue but greatly enhanced the production of labelled normetanaphrine.

When the animal experiment was done the other way round—noradrenaline injected intracisternally first and imipramine given later—the amounts of labelled noradrenaline and normetanephrine were both found increased in the brain, and it may be that imipramine and related tricyclic drugs decrease the rate of turnover of catecholamines.

In general the imipramine group of drugs is very safe and it is their atropine-like side effects of which patients usually complain. But there are situations in which they are potentially toxic. These are occasions where unusual amounts of amines are released and cannot be taken up again. Thus amphetamines cause amines to be released from their neuronal stores and as might be expected the tricyclic antidepressants potentiate the effects of amphetamines. They also enhance the effects of noradrenaline given intravenously. The really dangerous situation however is when a monoamine oxidase inhibitor is given first and one of the tricyclic drugs is added at a later date, and this reaction is quite comprehensible in terms of our neuronal model. Reserpine and imipramine have been given together in animals and in the therapeutic situation in man. However if the tricyclic drugs are given first and reserpine later this might give rise to behavioural excitability.

There are other hypotheses based on actions of imipramine

not involving amines. One suggests that imipramine functions by altering the properties of cell membranes. Imipramine and related compounds influence cell membranes rather in the same way that calcium does, stabilizing them and making them less permeable. Of course this is not incompatible with its action in limiting the reuptake of amines from the synaptic cleft.

Monoamine oxidase
inhibitors

As their name suggests monoamine oxidase inhibitors (MAOI) are compounds which block the group of enzymes known collectively as monoamine oxidase. According to one author monoamine oxidase may be responsible for destroying any amine synthesized in excess of storage capacity but this seems to be an oversimplified concept. If the enzyme monoamine oxidase is blocked by MAOI, concentrations of amines rise and levels of 2 or 3 times normal may be reached in the brain. Presumably most of this additional amine must be stored so the storage capacity cannot be strictly limited. We have also discussed the way in which the amine produced may control the formation of more by inhibiting a synthetic step, but this also does not seem to prevent amine levels in the brain and other tissues from rising when MAO is inhibited. Knowledge of what controls these dynamic equilibria under normal conditions and under both the influence of MAOI and of loading the brain with amino-acids or intermediate substances must await further work. Like imipramine MAOI can reverse reserpine-induced depression and the increase in the amounts of amines it produces in the brain are thought to be responsible for its antidepressant qualities. It is assumed that the increase in total brain concentrations is accompanied by greater availability of amine for physiological release and thus the end result with both MAOI and imipramine would be to subject the receptor to higher concentrations of physiologically active amine.

In animals it is possible to give large doses of a potent MAOI and to produce inhibition of the enzyme in a very short time indeed. In man this does not happen at therapeutic dosage. Work done on dying patients has shown quite clearly that inactivation of MAO and the resultant rise in the amount of 5-hydroxytryptamine in the brain did not occur until the patients had completed 2-3 weeks on MAOI. This more or less parallels the time relations of the clinical response to the drug.

Monoamine oxidase inhibitors have come into disrepute because they are powerful drugs which have been responsible for severe toxic actions. A number of foods such as certain cheeses, yeast extracts, and some wines, contain sufficient amines to affect the organism if they are not destroyed by MAO in the gut wall. When this enzyme is inhibited then this first line of defence is removed, and biologically active amines such as tyramine have been absorbed and been the cause of dangerous and sometimes fatal hypertensive crises. It is also possible that endogenously liberated amines could be harmful if allowed to accumulate, but drugs whose actions are normally limited by MAO are a much greater danger. The most dangerous substances are the sympathomimetic amines, which have been responsible for a number of severe reactions in patients who were taking MAOI.

It should be remembered that MAOI can be toxic in combination with imipramine as mentioned above, and also with reserpine. Animals who have been pretreated with MAOI and which therefore have increased levels of brain amines develop marked behavioural excitation and sometimes most serious toxic symptoms if given reserpine. Presumably this is due to the inability of the stores to hold the increased pools of amine. This effect is understandable in terms of our neuronal model.

Lithium

In the last five years two Danish workers have used lithium to prevent occurrence of affective disorders in patients who previously suffered from frequent relapses. In their hands a large number of patients did not experience further illness or had attenuated variants, and very few failed to benefit from this form of preventative treatment. This surely promises to be a valuable addition to our therapeutic armamentarium and a study of the physiological and biochemical effects of lithium may also increase our knowledge of the processes underlying the affective disorders.

Unfortunately although a lot of experiments have been done on animals in the past most of them have been performed using concentrations of lithium far in excess of those used in man for prophylaxis against affective illness. We know for instance that the sodium pump mechanism is unable to distinguish between sodium and lithium. It has been shown that at high concentrations of lithium the sodium pump is slowed and eventually comes to a stop but it is extremely unlikely that anything of this order is occurring at therapeutic dosages of lithium in man.

Here I will only discuss effects on amine metabolism though it is by no means established that lithium works completely or even partly on amines in the therapeutic situation. Quite recently a group of workers studied the behaviour of a fraction of brain homogenate derived from nerve endings. The brain homogenate came from rats, one group of which had been treated with lithium, and the fraction chosen was the one containing the intraneuronal structures which take up and store amine. They measured the amount of radioactive noradrenaline which was taken up by the homogenate from lithium-treated rats and compared it with that from control rats, and found an increased content of labelled amine in the lithium group. This suggested that the uptake mechanism was enhanced in these rats as compared to controls who had received no lithium.

In another centre the main catabolic products of noradrenaline were measured in the brain in lithium-treated rats. This was an *in vivo* experiment and it was found that there was an increase in the ratio of deaminated to O-methylated metabolites in these animals. Thus there was an increase in the metabolites derived from intracellular inactivation of noradrenaline and a decrease in the metabolites derived from released noradrenaline.

These two experiments support the view that lithium could decrease the activity of noradrenaline in the synaptic clefts by increasing reuptake. It is not known if increased reuptake applies to 5-hydroxytryptamine as well as to noradrenaline.

DOPA AND TRYPTOPHAN

Modifying the functions of enyzmes is not the only way of altering the amounts of amine in the brain. It is possible to increase the concentrations of an amine by providing large quantities of precursor amino-acid. An even greater increment is obtained if MAO is inhibited at the same time. This has been used to try to test the catecholamine hypothesis of depression on the theory that it may be possible to reverse the supposed bio-chemical defect—low catecholamines in the brain—by loading the patients with one of the catecholamine precursors. DL-Dopa was chosen and was given in oral doses of up to 1200 mg/day at about which level side effects began to be experienced by the patients.

Some of the patients were given MAOI as well as the amino-acid and a proportion of these developed transient hypertension. Rather disappointingly for the protagonists of this theory mood did not alter, but it is possible that insufficient dopa reached the brain to alter the gross amounts of noradrenaline. The experiment thus neither supports not refutes the hypothesis.

Other experiments have been done with tryptophan. Tryptophan in high doses by itself can cause psychological changes in normal individuals—chiefly sleepiness, feeling of drunkenness, euphoria and ataxia although some individuals complain of unpleasant feelings of unreality. Tryptophan was given in an attempt to potentiate the antidepressant effects of MAOI. Patients suffering from depression were given a month's treatment with MAOI and shortly afterwards they received either a large dose of DL-tryptophan (214 mg/kg body weight) or a placebo solution of similar taste and appearance. The results were both interesting and rather surprising.

The individuals who received tryptophan recovered more rapidly than the control subjects during the week they were taking the amino-acid, and thereafter they continued to improve at a comparatively accelerated rate. In a subsequent experiment the antidepressant action of tryptophan was compared with that of electroconvulsive therapy (E.C.T.). The dose of tryptophan was rather less than in the previous experiment and side effects were minimal. Taking the degree of recovery at 28 days as the criterion of efficacy treatment with tryptophan equalled that of E.C.T. although the initial response of E.C.T. was faster. There was a suggestion that the effects of tryptophan were slightly potentiated by MAOI but this was nothing like as obvious as the potentiation of MAOI by tryptophan.

It is very tempting to conclude from these precursor loading experiments that the amounts of 5-hydroxytryptamine in the brain in psychotic depression are of greater importance than the concentration of noradrenaline. This is both premature and over-simplified because although the initial effect of tryptophan loading is likely to be a rise in brain 5-hydroxytryptamine, this in itself is going to alter both the concentration and turnover of noradrenaline. Further study is needed to follow the various effects of amino-acid loading.

I think that this brief review shows how much progress has been made in our understanding of the actions of psychotropic drugs, but of course many of our present ideas may be erroneous. What is important is that a number of firm footholds have been established and further progress is to be expected with some confidence.

FURTHER READING

MICHAEL SHEPHERD, MALCOLM LADER and RICHARD RODNIGHT (1968) *Clinical Psychopharmacology*. English University Press, London.

Treatment of schizophrenia

F. J. J. LETEMENDIA
Littlemore Hospital,
Oxford

INTRODUCTION

Schizophrenia still remains a vague and ill-defined illness. In large measure the lack of clarity can be traced back to the origins of the concept.

Kraepelin very successfully applied the idea of the disease entity, taken from general medicine, to the study of the major organic psychoses. The requirements for inclusion in the entity were: an established cause, the same symptoms, evolution, end state and post-mortem findings. Dementia praecox, the parent concept of schizophrenia, followed the model of the disease entity although imperfectly. Little was known about the cause and the post-mortem findings were inconclusive; the only remaining support for the entity was the evolution towards end states characterized by a dementia *sui generis*.

For E. Bleuler, the originator of the term schizophrenia, attention was concentrated not on the evolution but on the psychological symptoms that lead to dementia. His definition of the symptoms that were always present and characteristic of schizophrenia, the 'fundamental' symptoms, and those that originated from the disease process and were termed 'primary' placed the diagnosis of the condition on the psychological plane. He continued to accept that schizophrenia was incurable and ended in deterioration.

However the concept of schizophrenia was much wider than that of dementia praecox alone and included states that shaded imperceptibly into the schizoid personality and into normality. It also comprised conditions that subsequently showed a complete recovery, with *restitutio ad integrum*.

Kraepelin though an expert in botany was far from being the rigid taxonomist he is made out to have been. With an uncommon flexibility of mind, six years before his death he abandoned the frame he had so patiently erected. In his last paper in 1920 he said: 'Repeatedly the thought has been expressed lately that research in clinical psychiatry has come to a halt. The method of considering causes, symptoms, course and end state, as well as post-mortem findings to define forms of illness has become stale and cannot satisfy any longer: new ways must be found. One cannot deny a certain justification for statements of this kind.' He then goes on to criticize his previous position and he ends by adopting one very close to that of his great adversary Hoche. Instead of the nosological unit he encourages research on individual factors like age, sex, race, education and other environmental factors that shape mental disease.

In Britain Kraepelin's last paper has received little or no attention. The translation of 'Dementia Praecox' from his textbook, the eighth German edition of 1913, was published in Edinburgh in 1925. Thus his older views formed the basis of the teaching of dementia praecox in Britain as can be seen in Henderson and Gillespie's textbook (1956).

As a result of Bleuler's change of criteria a double way of thinking was maintained about schizophrenia and still persists. On the one hand dementia praecox is a deteriorating disease, on the other schizophrenia is an often curable condition with ill-defined boundaries with other illnesses and with normality. Some, dissatisfied with the dilemma, advocated a return to the old concept of 'dementia praecox' and the use of evolution towards dementia as the separating criterion. Others divided schizophrenia into a nuclear group with bad prognosis and a marginal one with favourable outcome. Langfeldt's schizophrenia proper and schizophreniform illnesses and the 'genuine' and 'pseudo'-schizophrenia of Rumke reflect this dual conception.

A further difficulty remained: predictions of outcome based on the presenting symptoms were of no clear value in clinical practice. The best study up to 1930 was that of Mauz in Kretschmer's school. He studied 1500 cases of functional psychoses and tried to relate to prognosis phenomenological information and observations on somatotypes. No clear-cut practical guidelines emerged and few clinical workers would fare well in predicting outcome using the criteria given by Mauz.

Mayer-Gross summarized the literature on prognosis until 1932. Until then nobody considered treatment was of much use in affecting prognosis. Bleuler had flatly asserted that there was no treatment. Mayer-Gross in about 800 pages on schizophrenia in Bumke's *Handbook* devoted only nine to the subject of treatment.

Early physical methods of treatment

In this confused state about the diagnosis and prognosis of schizophrenia the first of the physical methods of treatment made its appearance. It was in 1933 that von Meduna advanced the mistaken notion of the antagonism between schizophrenia and epilepsy and advocated the treatment of the former with metrazol-induced convulsions. This spasmodic start was to open the present era of therapeutic enthusiasm. Its history is by now familiar. In 1935 Sakel introduced insulin coma therapy (I.C.T.): in 1937 Cerletti and Bini devized a method for the electrical induction of convulsions (E.C.T.). The former became the main treatment of schizophrenia and the latter found its target in the treatment of mood disorders.

I.C.T. was of limited application. In part it required special facilities and highly trained nursing and medical personnel; but also it was thought that only those cases which had been ill for less than two years had the best outcome. Assessment of results can be found in the textbooks of the time and reflect general optimism. The failure rate in a properly selected population was 34% according to Bumke. Claims about the resulting transformation of institutional life are reminiscent of those made today. Thus Bumke says: 'It is now a long time since patients smeared their faces and drank their urine, their violence has been reduced and they have suffered less from hallucinations'.

Those patients ill for more than two years were on the whole not treated with I.C.T. and it was not until E. Moniz and A. Lima devised the leucotomy operation that they were reached by the therapeutic wave. It was stated that one third of such chronic patients could thus be brought to the point where they could live in the community but it is not easy to forget the crudity of the initial attempts and the suffering they produced, which has been in large measure the reason for the decline of brain surgery in the treatment of schizophrenia.

Early psychological treatment

Although E. Bleuler conceived the illness as largely incurable he was particularly interested in the psychological mechanisms involved. Together with Jung he tried psychoanalytic methods at the Burghölzli with no evident success and he held the view, as Freud did, that schizophrenics presented particular difficulties in the development of the transference. When it appeared it was different from that obtaining in the neuroses and resulted in pathological love, occasionally followed by persecutory ideas of a sexual nature. Since Freud there has been a positive discouragement to those embarking on psychotherapy of the psychoses on the grounds that in borderline cases such therapy could release the illness while aggravating it in those already manifestly ill. However E. Bleuler did not abandon psychological principles of management of a general kind. He observed that the majority of the symptoms were secondary i.e. not directly arising from the process itself, and many could be easily removed. Catatonic manifestation often disappeared through re-education, sometimes by firm handling, sometimes by patient understanding. Smearing and other undesirable habits could be removed by simple procedures. By appropriate drill he noted it was possible to change behaviour. 'In this manner the patients can be brought to the point where they will do the correct thing either mechanically or out of habit.' He pursued vigorously the prevention of autism by occupation and frequent changes of environment. He stated that he was 'well acquainted with the almost incorrigible products of the isolation cells of many hospitals.' His attitude about admission is very close to that encouraged today. He advised against admission simply on the grounds of diagnosis but only when the schizophrenic was dangerous or when he presented a threat to the well-being of the healthy members of the family and it was no longer possible to influence him. As soon as re-education had occurred, early discharge, even before a 'cure', achieved better results.

Other than these general precepts interest in psychotherapy was overshadowed by the active pursuit of physical therapies. Bumke dismisses psychotherapy in one sentence of his textbook. American psychiatry was more prepared by A. Mayer's psychobiological approach to consider the importance of psychological factors in the aetiology of schizophrenia. A. Brill (1929) concerned himself with the applications of psychoanalysis to psychiatry, in particular to the treatment of schizophrenics, and the efforts of W. C. Menninger (1932) went towards the application of psychotherapeutic methods in the psychiatric hospital. From then on there was continuous interest and no reserve in approaching schizophrenic patients with psychotherapy.

Occupational therapy

H. Simon described in 1927 the results of his *aktivere therapie* in the mental hospital at Gütersloh. He accepted current ideas that the illness was the result of an organic process and he aimed at modifying not the process but the marginal manifestations or 'institutional artefacts' by means mainly of agricultural and domestic manual work but also by other more general changes in social milieu.

Carl Schneider postulated that in schizophrenia there were symptoms, complexes, or syndromes which had a biological basis and he claimed to have discovered empirically that some responded differently to the biological therapies then available. Thus the syndrome of 'thought withdrawal' responded to work therapy, whereas that of 'drivelling' was susceptible to I.C.T. These ideas although attractive and original have not received confirmation. They are reminiscent of current attempts at defining the target symptoms in drug therapy.

MODERN PHYSICAL METHODS

Two discoveries contributed to the abandonment of I.C.T. The first was the advent of the phenothiazines introduced by Delay and Deniker in 1952. Although initially used in the control of psychomotor overactivity it was soon claimed that the beneficial effects went beyond this and that by reducing anxiety and preoccupation they reduced other psychotic symptoms in schizophrenia e.g. delusional ideas. As a form of treatment the phenothiazines, unlike I.C.T., were easy to apply and they did not require teams of nursing and medical experts. The indications soon extended to all schizophrenics, acute and chronic.

The second was the demonstration by Ackner, Harris and Oldham of the lack of specificity of I.C.T. A comparison between I.C.T. and barbiturate-induced coma in two randomly selected groups of patients showed there were no significant differences in outcome either immediately after treatment or three years later. I.C.T. has virtually ceased as a form of treatment in schizophrenia.

The phenothiazines are now universally used. Contrary to the rigid method for I.C.T. there is no single policy for the way they are given. Any drug may be used and there is considerable variation in dosage and duration of treatment. In spite of an enormous literature few claims about their efficacy have been established beyond doubt. Chlorpromazine is still the most widely used in dosage, ranging between 75 to 3,000 mgm. a day. That chlorpromazine markedly reduces psychomotor activity is well established in a number of well-controlled observations. More difficult to demonstrate is its effect on schizophrenic states.

The largest and best controlled experiment with phenothiazines in acute schizophrenia is the collaborative study conducted by the National Institute of Mental Health and the Psychopharmacology Service Center in nine hospitals in the U.S.A. Over 400 patients were treated in random allocation to one of four treatments: fluphenazine ('moditen'), thioridazine ('melleril'), chlorpromazine ('largactil', 'thorazine', 'megaphen', etc.) and placebo. Ninety-five per cent of drug treated patients showed some degree of improvement within six weeks, over 75% showed marked to moderate degrees of improvement. In comparison over half the schizophrenics treated with placebo showed some improvement but only 23% were rated markedly or moderately improved. At the end of six weeks 46% of those on drugs were rated as having no or only minimal symptoms. An important finding was the absence of significant differences in efficacy among the phenothiazines used in the trial. In view of this thioridazine should be the drug of choice in the treatment of acute cases because of the low incidence of undesirable effects.

As yet there is no clear evidence of how long treatment should continue after the acute symptoms are controlled. Since episodic schizophrenia is common (about 45% of cases according to M. Bleuler) it would be predicted that a good number of such patients would remain well if the drug were withdrawn. However a usual practice is to keep a maintenance dose for long periods of time, often years. Whether this prevents relapses is not easy to demonstrate in the absence of prognostic indications of relapse for the individual patient and the lack of properly controlled comparisons between medicated and non-medicated groups.

In the treatment of chronic schizophrenia the practice for most patients is to maintain them indefinitely on phenothiazines. Prolonged administration has brought to the fore fresh undesirable effects of these drugs, to be added to those such as parkinsonism, jaundice, agranulocytosis already known after short-term administration. Those recently reported are deposits of pigment in the eye, skin, and internal organs, and there are some cases of unexplained sudden death in patients on phenothiazines for long periods where post-mortem reveals visceral pigmentation.

The efficacy of the phenothiazines in chronic schizophrenia is generally accepted but the experimental evidence for this is not so easy to obtain. Withdrawal of the drug and substitution by a placebo in some cases results in relapse, which may occur any time between a few weeks and six months. The proportions relapsing vary between 19% and 45%; Hughes and Crawford Little have recently reviewed the literature. The gap between discontinuation of the drug and relapse has made some adopt an intermittent pattern of administration with rests of two weeks every four to six weeks. The risk here is the patient's discontinuation of therapy.

That a substantial number of patients do not regularly take drugs prescribed for them has been shown by several workers. Unless urine checks are introduced it is impossible to know whether the patient's unimproved mental state means lack of efficacy of the drug or failure to take it. Hare and Wilcox have found that about 50% of psychiatric out-patients, 37% of day patients and 19% of in-patients do not take what is prescribed.

A new method of phenothiazine therapy is that of intramuscular injection of fluphenazine enanthate (one ml. = 25 mgm.) every two to three weeks. Initially, until the way in which the patient tolerates the side effects is established supervision preferably in hospital is desirable. Some complain of marked extrapyramidal symptoms between one and three days after the injection. Once the requirements of anti-parkinsonian drugs have been adjusted the routine injection is a much simpler

method than conventional oral administration of other phenothiazines given in once or thrice daily schedules. Supervision in
out-patients can be carried out by senior nurses at a follow-up
clinic. Other than saving nursing time an important advantage
of fluphenazine enanthate is the certainty that the patient is
having the medication prescribed.

Haloperidol, ('serenace'), a butyrophenone, was introduced as
a neuroleptic in 1960. It has indications very similar to those of
the phenothiazines. In a recent symposium J. Cole summarized
the virtues of the drug: it is an effective neuroleptic with hyper-
active patients and it has an equivocal or possibly good effect
on more conventional schizophrenic phenomena like paranoid
delusions and hallucinations. It is too early to say whether it is
more effective than the phenothiazines. G. C. Crane reviewed
the available literature. The dosage varied between 1-200 mg.
a day with a median of 15 mg. a day. (Dosages in continental
reports tend to be on average lower than 15 mg. per day). As
to side effects there is no advantage over the phenothiazines in
using haloperidol. Extrapyramidal symptoms appear as frequently and we do not yet know, because the experience with the
drug is still scanty, what the effects of long-term administration
are likely to be.

A. Hoffer et al. have claimed that nicotinic acid or nicotinamide, in daily mega doses of 3-18 gm. over a period of 33 days,
are effective in most forms of schizophrenia. They can be used in
conjunction with other treatments. The evidence on the clinical
effectiveness is of an indirect kind, i.e. reduction of stay in
hospital and lessening of the relapse rate. A controlled independent study by N. Kline et al. showed no difference between treatment and placebo. In view of this more studies are required
before the claim can be accepted.

E.C.T. has been used increasingly in acute and chronic forms
of schizophrenia in conjunction with phenothiazines and other
drugs. The main indications are: catatonic symptoms particularly
stupor (which often respond to a few treatments), and the severe

forms of catatonia described by Stauder, where repeated daily applications of E.C.T. are said to be life-saving; also mood disorders in schizophrenia—depressive states, delusional moods, and states where perplexity is dominant. Some have advocated maintenance E.C.T. in chronic patients who show a tendency to lethargy or periods of withdrawn behaviour.

MODERN PSYCHOLOGICAL TREATMENT

The forties saw a spread of interest in the psychodynamics of schizophrenia at a time when the field was taken up by biological methods of treatment; some attempts were made at psychotherapy (Federn, 1943) but none had the dramatic impact of the methods of direct analysis introduced by J. A. Rosen (1946). He claimed that by direct and forceful interpretation contact could be established with withdrawn schizophrenics and the illness could be rapidly cured. The old difficulty of the transference had been overcome and the results of treatment were favourable. No doubt Rosen's impact contributed to stimulation of interest and encouraged others to try more thoughtful psychoanalytic techniques. The number of papers on the subject increased and many were critical of Rosen's methods and conclusions; the transference was possible but it was of a very delicate nature compared with that obtaining in the neuroses. The counter-transference and the personality of the therapist were again of much greater importance than in the neuroses. Frieda Fromm-Reichman (1952) did not accept that Rosen's patients were cured, but only no longer psychotic, and she remarked that on his own admission they were handed over to another therapist once they attained this state.

Most of the attempts until then had been with acute schizophrenics and it was remarked that to claim 'cures' might be misleading since many such patients often showed spontaneous remissions. The criteria for cure in psychotherapy of schizophrenia should in fact be restitution to normal ego function and not disappearance of symptoms, as for the physical treatments (Eisler, 1952). Subsequent work by Horwitz et al. found that 19 out of the 37 patients originally treated by Rosen could still be traced. Seven were not schizophrenics (six neurotic and one manic depressive) and the twelve remaining were far from cured and had required long periods in hospital and much physical treatment.

Although there has been continuing interest and much has been learned about the mechanisms and difficulties involved in the psychotherapy of schizophrenia, chronic patients still present a formidable undertaking, and only few people of those with adequate training possess the virtues of personality, persistence and patience needed for the task. Nobody now claims rapid cures, and in view of the numbers of patients in need of treatment analytical psychotherapy for the majority remains unimportant in practice. Even given the facilities for psychotherapy a comparative trial of psychoanalytic psychotherapy, drugs, and a combination of the two, in which the patients were allocated randomly to each of the three treatments, proved that drugs did significantly better, whether alone or together with psychotherapy than psychotherapy alone.

There has been increasing attention paid to group treatment methods. They represent an economy of effort and skilled manpower. Moreno (1945) introduced psychodrama and claimed as a result that individual methods would no longer be required. There are surveys of the literature on group therapy of the psychoses by Gurri and Chasen and Gifford and Mackenzie. Frank conducted a rather loosely controlled experiment with 174 chronic schizophrenic patients, 118 of which were allocated to small groups of 10-15 patients for psychotherapy while the remainder formed the control group. No significant differences were observed between the groups, although in the first year the psychotherapy groups showed deterioration in terms of more aggressive destructive behaviour while in the second year there was improvement when compared with the control group.

However from the events reported in his paper many factors that affected patients and staff could not be adequately controlled. The value of group methods in the treatment of chronic schizophrenia is not yet established because of the lack of properly controlled studies.

Community, milieu and administrative therapies

It is unfortunate from the point of view of assessment of the effects of treatment that both the chemotherapies and administrative reforms were introduced about the same time. An extensive and vigorous literature has developed in defence of the merits of one or other of these ways of treatment. There is little chance of resolving the problem. Although there are indications that administrative changes in England preceded drug therapy, as Shepherd and others have shown by the analysis of hospital statistics, by and large the effects appear cumulative and complementary. The drugs are said to have helped at two levels, making the patients more accessible and the staff more confident in the adoption of liberal and more humane policies in administration.

Assessment of drug effects are difficult, as any cursory survey of the literature shows, but the concepts of administrative and community therapies present almost unsurmountable difficulties in research. D. Clark has described some of the complexities in the concepts and attempted measurements of changes in patients under therapy, but these are still descriptive rather than analytical.

Rehabilitation

Simon's efforts to remove by his *aktivere therapie* the artefacts produced by inactivity in the mental state of patients and in the minds of staff are the seed of those devoted at present to removing handicaps which delay or prevent rehabilitation.

By far the most extensive, careful and systematic work has been that carried out by the M.R.C. Social Psychiatry Research

Unit at the Maudsley Hospital. O'Connor et al. studied the work performance of chronic schizophrenics as assessed by output and determined in an objective way and found that some normal incentives like money or encouragement had little effect. Wing et al. studied the effect of an Industrial Rehabilitation Unit (I.R.U.) on 45 moderately handicapped male schizophrenic patients who had been in hospital for more than two years. They found that one year after discharge 11 patients were working satisfactorily in open industry and a further 10 in sheltered employment. The remainder were unemployed. All patients remained handicapped in some way although some showed minimal disability. At least 6 patients became severely ill while at the I.R.U., and 10 more showed a milder form of adverse reaction. As a result of their work they conclude that: 'About 23% of the chronic schizophrenic patients in hospitals in England and Wales might be expected to be satisfactorily settled in employment one year after completing an I.R.U. course.' A further 22% could be settled in Remploy factories.

It is evident from their work that considerable effort and care went into the selection and preparation for rehabilitation of at least some of the patients. Less determined efforts and inadequacies in after-care and support while the patient is trying to establish himself in the community may lead to poor results in rehabilitation. Some of these patients need constant help and encouragement and the facilities available in the community leave much to be desired.

An attempt to rehabilitate the chronic patient at the mental hospital has been demonstrated by Early in Bristol. Progress upwards occurs in two not necessarily parallel ladders: domestic resettlement moves along progressive graded steps from improved wards to hostel accommodation, towards ultimate independent life in the community; rehabilitation in work, towards economic independence, is induced by creating conditions increasingly comparable to industry outside. Industrial work under contract started in Bristol in 1950. The next step was the creation of the

Industrial Therapy Organization (Bristol) Ltd., (I.T.O.), a non-profit making company in which patients are considered as self-employed, doing piece-work. Also under the cover of the I.T.O. there are sheltered work facilities and self-supporting work like a car-washing service. A further and interesting development of Early's work is the placement of groups of patients in factories outside. Efforts of a less structured character and on a smaller scale to rehabilitate chronic patients are nowadays to be seen in many hospitals for the mentally ill.

Summary

The difficulties in the assessment of treatment for schizophrenia are closely bound to the uncertainties in the diagnosis and outcome of this illness.

Psychological treatments are of considerable theoretical interest. They have contributed to a better understanding of those factors in the environment that may affect the disease. Individual psychotherapy is complex and time-consuming, and in consequence of very limited use in the treatment of the majority of hospital patients. Group methods, because of their economy, have a wider application

Drug therapy is easy to administer and is employed on a large scale. Its usefulness has been demonstrated in acute schizophrenic patients, and there is considerable evidence that it is also helpful in chronic states.

Rehabilitation is a major tool in reducing disability, particularly in chronic schizophrenia.

REFERENCES

KRAEPELIN E. (1920) Forms of presentation of mental illness. *Z. ges. Neurol. Psychiat.* **62**, 1. 256-510.

MAUZ F. (1930) *The prognosis of endogenous psychoses.* Thieme, Leipzig.

MAYER-GROSS W. (1932) *Schizophrenia.* In Bumke's Handbook of Mental Diseases. Vol. **9**, Berlin.

BUMKE O. (1941) *Textbook of Mental Diseases.* Fifth edition, Munich.

ACKNER B., HARRIS A., and OLDHAM A. J. (1957) Insulin treatment of Schizophrenia. *Lancet*, I, 607-611.

N.I.M.H.—P.R.B. Collaborative Study Group (1964) Phenothiazine Treatment in Acute Schizophrenia. *Arch gen. Psychiat.* 10, 246-261.

GOOD W. W., STERLING M. and HOLZMAN W. H. (1958) Termination of chlorpromazine with schizophrenic patients *Amer. J. Psychiat.* 115, 443-448.

DIAMOND L. S. and MARKS J. B. (1960) Discontinuance of tranquillizers among chronic schizophrenic patients receiving maintenance drugs. *J. nerv. ment. Dis.* 131, 247-251.

HUGHES J. S. and CRAWFORD LITTLE J. (1967) An appraisal of the continuing practice of prescribing tranquillizing drugs for long stay psychiatric patients. *Brit. J. Psychiat.* 113, 867-873.

HARE E. H. and WILLCOX D. R. C. (1967) Do psychiatric in-patients take their pills? *Brit. J. Psychiat.* 113, 1435-1439.

COLE J. O. (1967) Concluding remarks and summary. *International J. Neuropsychiat.* 3, Supp. I. 150-152.

CRANE G. E. (1967) A review of clinical literature on Haloperidol. *International J. Neuropsvchiat.* 3, Supp. I. 110-123.

HOFFER A., OSMOND H., CALLBECK M. J. and KAHAN I. (1957) Treatment of schizophrenia with nicotinic acid and nicotinamide. *J. Clin. Exp. psychopathol.* 18, 131-158.

KLINE N., BARCLAY G. L., COLE J. O., ESSER A. H., LEHMANN H. and WITTENBORN, J. R. (1967) Controlled evaluation of nicotinamide adenine dinucleotide in the treatment of chronic schizophrenic patients. *Brit. J. Psychiat.* 113, 731-742.

HORWITZ W. A., POLATIN P., KOLB L. C. and HOCH P. H. (1957) A study of cases of schizophrenia treated by 'direct analysis'. *Amer. J. Psychiat.* 114, 780-783.

MAY P. R. A. and TUMA A. H. (1965) Treatment of schizophrenia. An experimental study of five treatment methods. *Brit. J. Psychiat.* 111, 503-510.

GURRIE J. and CHASEN M. (1948) Preliminary survey of the results of group therapy of psychoses *Dis. Nerv. System.* 9, 52-54.

GIFFORD S. and MACKENZIE J. (1948) A review of the literature on group therapy of psychoses. *Dis. Nerv. System.* 9, 19-24.

FRANK J. (1952) Group psychotherapy in chronic schizophrenia in *Psychotherapy with schizophrenics*. Ed. Brody E. and Redlich E. Inter. Univ. Press. New York.

CLARK D. H. (1966) The therapeutic community. Concept, practice and future. *Brit. J. Psychiat.* 111, 947-954.

O'CONNOR N., HERON A. and CARSTAIRS G. M. (1956) Work performance of chronic schizophrenics. *Occup. Psychol.* **30**, 153.

WING J. K., BENNETT D. H. and DENHAM J. *The Industrial Rehabilitation of Long-stay Schizophrenic patients.* Medical Research Council Report N.42. London H.M.S.O.

EARLY D. F. (1965) Domestic resettlement. Economic rehabilitation. In *Psychiatric Hospital Care.* Ed. Freeman H., Baillière, Tindall and Cassell. London.

Treatment of epilepsy

DAVID C. TAYLOR

Park Hospital,
Oxford

What constitutes treatment is about as difficult to define as epilepsy itself. Most people agree that epilepsy is not a disease, not even a unitary disorder, yet illogically the notion persists that a paper with such a title as this has a value.

Epilepsy is a unifying behavioural concept of doubtful heuristic value, a vague nosological entity like cough, or limp, or even schizophrenia. The form of the disorder is widely various, from dramatic motor threshings in cyanosed unconsciousness to the sudden collapse of the akinetic seizure or the blank absence in true petit mal. At times in psychomotor epilepsy it is no more than the moment of foolishness of ambiguous origin. The causes of the disorder are also widely various, often composite, and usually concealed. The nature of the incapacities is diverse—intellectual, psychological, social and physical. The danger of the attacks is diverse, and in order of increasing frequency come status epilepticus, which may cause death; the risk of serious accident, through falls, through machines, through drowning; and psychological effects, stigma, social failure, mental disorder and suicide.

It is however probably statistically true that the majority of people who suffer some epileptic attacks will, through drugs and regimes, find a full and normal life perfectly possible. This should be borne in mind though such persons do not in the main present the major therapeutic challenge.

111

AIMS OF TREATMENT

The aims of treatment are:

(i) To make the best possible ascertainment of causative factors, to discover any remediable causes, and relieve them.

(ii) Through knowledge of the causes of epilepsy to prevent it where possible, for example by improved genetic counselling, obstetrics and paediatrics.

(iii) To reduce to a minimum, in the light of other therapeutic considerations, the frequency or likelihood of potentially dangerous epileptic attacks.

(iv) To make a thorough assessment of the intellectual, psychological, social and physical handicaps liable to accompany the epilepsy, or the cerebral dysfunction which this implies, or the structural damage which may underlie the dysfunction, or the disorder which may be responsible for the cerebral damage, and to mitigate these handicaps as far as possible.

(v) To make thorough assessment of the psychiatric and social effects on the patient of a chronic socially disadvantageous disorder and to modify these effects.

(vi) To become acquainted with abnormal conditions in the patients' milieu and abnormal attitudes in his intimates and to alter them.

Treatment so broadly based as this is only likely to be possible in the type of centre envisaged by the Cohen Report (1956).

CLINICAL APPROACH

Investigation

The physician faced with an epileptic person to treat will have in mind the improbability of his discovering an obvious remediable cause for the disorder, such as a cerebral tumour, hypoglycaemia, hypercalcaemia, or lead poisoning, but through a thorough biography, history and examination he will usually attempt to ascertain the aetiology of the epilepsy. The extent to which he will pursue his investigations will very properly depend on a number of factors.

Prime amongst these will be the frequency of the attacks. The occasional convulsion under special circumstances is so common that not every individual who suffers a convulsion merits full investigation or demands treatment on this criterion alone. Then there is the duration of the attack. Brief episodes may be hardly incapacitating but prolonged or serially repeated convulsions demand urgent termination and subsequent careful supervision. The form of the attacks will influence therapeutic attitude. Where a minor fluctuation of consciousness may be considered of little importance a bizarre seizure with a complex socially embarrassing automatism will cause more concern. Finally at times the nature of the attack, for example partial continual epilepsy, may suggest immediate investigation.

However over-enthusiastic investigation is not indicated. The majority of routine clinical investigations will prove negative, which may lead through disappointment to clinical apathy and to the assumption that the condition is idiopathic (which is a diagnosis by exclusion), and on the other hand a diligent search for causes must extend across a vast range of possibilities. It is more prudent and more rewarding to adhere to the well-established discipline of the clinical history than to fire off a random volley of special investigations. Even so there is a temptation to emphasize facile explanations such as a history of abnormal birth, trauma or infection, and to miss the significance of factors more subtle but more contemporary and more pertinent.

Clinical history

A good clinical history will include an account of the *first* observed attack. The age at which this occurred is of critical significance. It sets a limit to the time of operation of the primary aetiological factor and determines the point in the ontogeny when the patient was affected, a factor which will modify his development, maturity, and social achievement from then on. It may differ by years from the onset of *habitual* seizures.

The circumstances of the attack, whether preceded by fever, whether in sleep or awake, whether in relationship to unusual stimuli, will vary the aetiological and therapeutic possibilities. The nature, duration, and treatment of the first attack need to be known since cerebral scarification may follow uncontrolled early status epilepticus and such prolonged seizures are too often dismissed as 'febrile convulsions' (Ounsted, Lindsay and Norman, 1966). The nature of current attacks should be described both by the patient and by others. Informants will describe the attacks adequately if they are allowed to do so. The psychiatrist should be master of this technique of enquiry, but too often the patient is inhibited by embarrassment or by the brevity of this part of the interview from recounting weird and apparently idiosyncratic epileptic experience.

Localisation

Since therapeutic possibilities will depend on the area of brain affected by the seizure the aim is to attempt to locate this. Elegant associations between behaviour observable during drug-induced seizures and cerebral localisation of the disturbance have been described.

The temporal sequence of events may suggest the area in which the attack originated. The clearest examples come from patients with focal disturbance in the motor areas who may recall gradually spreading clonic movements or paresis at the onset of the attack. The equivalent sensory phenomena are less evident, probably because they are subjectively trivial compared with the motor component. Disturbances of the special sensory apparatus, with the exception of visual phenomena of the hemianopic type, are by virtue of their bilateral representation of less localising value.

The most commonly reported sensory disturbances which presage or accompany a fit are those arising from the temporal lobe. Classically these are olfactory and gustatory but the frequency of autonomic sensory phenomena far exceeds them. The autonomic sensations include the epigastric rush, described as 'like being on a big dipper' or 'butterflies in the stomach' but often confused with 'wind' or 'indigestion' or even 'ulcer pain'. Various other sensations of asphyxia, of nausea, or palpitations, might be mistaken for anxiety; and rectal or penile sensations with erection may be misinterpreted as masturbation, especially in the young or the psychotic (Gastaut, 1953).

Careful work has illustrated that profound observable autonomic changes do occur peripherally during the attack and one might wonder with James and Lange about the true nature of the fear which so commonly occurs (Williams, 1956) as it were autochthonously. In this unique situation there is no external stimulus for the fear response and the sensation could merely be the patient's interpretation of the sudden autonomic changes. Such phenomena may be inferred at times from behaviour. For example the child who blanches, who seems transfixed by fear, who suddenly rushes to mother, and who herself reports palpitations preceding the convulsive movements may be assumed to be experiencing the limbic type of attack originally described by Hippocrates. There are complex behavioural aspects to these attacks. The strange automatisms include chewing, drooling, groping, drinking, smoking, undressing. Patients describe feelings of strangeness and familiarity, intrusive thought, thought blocking, two lines of thought, and perversions of memory, as well as variability in the quality and size of perception of the self and the environment.

Some types of epilepsy accompanied by focal abnormalities in the EEG may have a focal basis, but the occurrence of generalised attacks does not preclude a focal pathology. Any central structure, focally damaged, could be responsible not only for a generalised attack but also for the generalised EEG abnormalities. The most clearly generalised attacks are those of petit mal. These are usually reported as moments of vagueness or dreaminess or inattention, as if in a moving picture the projector had stuck at a frame for a few seconds before moving on. Movement at such times is largely confined to the eyes rolling, staring, or blinking, and if posture is maintained the observer emphasizes the failure of sensory input. Alternatively posture may fail (the akinetic attack) or myoclonus be evident. Major convulsive attacks and the massive spasms of the salaam attacks are both accompanied by widely generalised electrical disturbances.

Considerable evidence is now available that careful psychological testing is of value in helping to localise areas of cerebral damage, but the handedness of the patient needs to be known. Furthermore this accurate knowledge of reductions in specific abilities will be required in guiding the patient's education and occupation.

Aetiology

A search for aetiological clues should cover the whole biography for in epilepsy much time may pass between the insult and the seizure response. However, the causes may not be evident. The occurrence of epileptic attacks in some people merely draws attention to their abnormal cerebral function. This abnormality could be statistical in the sense that while most people do not convulse there are some at the extreme of normal variation who do, in which case the condition is neither symptom nor disease. More likely it is individual, in the sense that something is causing a person who would not normally convulse to do so, a reaction which ought to be considered as absolutely pathological.

Heredity: That there may be in some people a predisposition to convulsion at least in early life is suggested by the genetics of febrile convulsions. In the siblings of probands who are selected on the basis of febrile convulsions the frequency of convulsions is very high (Ounsted, Lindsay and Norman, 1966). Febrile convulsions are themselves of frequent occurrence and they have a powerful genetic link. This suggests that the majority of those afflicted survive sufficiently intact to perpetuate the gene. Some work also suggests hereditary predisposition to centrencephalic epilepsy and focal temporal lobe abnormalities.

Some epilepsy arises through dominant or recessive genes

responsible for cerebral disorders such as tuberose sclerosis or phenylketonuria or the cerebellar degenerations. The possibility of more subtle hereditary influences is suggested by the frequency with which serious disturbance in the family (by psychopathic disorder, alcoholism, or other severe social maladjustment) is found in the history in some series of seriously incapacitated epileptics. (Ounsted, Lindsay and Norman, 1966; Taylor and Falconer, 1968). These disturbances may of course be environmental.

Environment: On the patient himself such family disturbance may of course itself have a provocative effect and the good effect of removing an epileptic to a more serene and ordered environment often suggests the importance of this. Psychological influences such as parental discord or bereavement or a family member with mental illness should be considered (Dominian et al. 1963). The effect of these variables on the degree of incapacity of patients with temporal lobe epilepsy treated by surgery was considerable (Taylor and Falconer, 1968).

Pregnancy: Enquiry should be made into the mother's obstetric history. What risks arose? For example, did she have rubella, what was the likelihood of syphilis or any other transmittable disease? Complications of the pregnancy such as vomiting, bleeding or toxaemia and their management should be noted though the relationship of each to specific late handicap is not yet known.

The mother's management of her pregnancy reflects her ability to care for herself, her attitude to the pregnancy, and perhaps her attitude to the child. Her postpartum mental state may suggest that the child was neglected, mismanaged, even battered.

Delivery: The weight and gestational age of the infant should be known. There are two broad classes of small infants, those who are premature (short gestation) and at risk for anoxic damage and those whose growth was retarded in utero and who are at risk for hypoglyceamia. Both these complications require urgent therapeutic intervention if the brain is to survive intact.

Abnormal presentation and instrumental birth probably increase the risk to the child. In one series breech birth was much commoner than usual in patients with centrencephalic epilepsy with spike and wave EEG abnormality. If there is anything at all to the story that cerebral compression in the birth canal produces incisural sclerosis, which is doubtful, then it ought to be more evident in the biggest child to pass through a given pelvis, but there is no evidence that this is so.*

An abnormal child may declare itself at or before birth by causing concern through foetal distress, cyanotic attacks, undue drowsiness, or fits. Later these signs are often taken to imply 'difficult labour' which is then considered aetiological in the child's abnormality, at least by the mother, but this need not be true. The best evidence is the actual notes of the delivery, and the surest sign of real anxiety at that time is that the infant was separated from the mother and treated.

Early infancy: Infection and pyrexia are the greatest epileptogenic hazards of early infancy. Meningitis, encephalitis, or abscess are the most damaging but damage sustained during other infections is more frequent. This damage results because pyrexia with its attendant metabolic changes leads to prolonged uncontrolled convulsions, which make enormous demands on cerebral metabolism, needing extra oxygen at a time when the convulsive movements are embarrassing respiratory function. Anoxic cerebral damage strikes certain specially sensitive areas such as the mesial temporal structures, where scarring can be highly epileptogenic. Such mesial temporal sclerosis is evident in about half the cases of temporal lobe epilepsy examined pathologically or neurosurgically. Direct damage from the infective process may also produce scarring.

The other risks in early infancy are cerebral trauma, which may be accidental when it will be described however trivial, or deliberate when it will be concealed if possible however violent. Intoxications and metabolic disorders complete the list of

*See Earle et al., (1953) and Falconer and Taylor, (1968).

important risks. Cerebral tumour should always be borne in mind though the majority of infantile tumours are infratentorial and not highly epileptogenic.

DRUG TREATMENT

It is taken as a *sine qua non* in the therapeutics of epilepsy that drug treatment is indicated to reduce the frequency of attacks. Whilst the physical dangers of the attacks have been outlined and are real, there are other components of epileptic incapacity. Consequently any therapeutic regime must be shown to produce not only a real decrease in attacks but also a decrease in incapacity. The wisest course is to understand a few of the wide range of drugs available. There is no panacea. Excellent summaries of anti-convulsants, their actions and their unwanted effects are available in the literature ('Today's Drugs'). A few drugs will be outlined here. No doses will be quoted. The rule is to medicate with as small an amount, of as few drugs as possible, given as seldom daily as their metabolism will allow.

Phenobarbitone is the oldest and cheapest remedy and it may be tried in any type of seizure. It is a sedative but it is safe since it rarely produces systemic mischief. In children it will often increase incapacity by provoking a wide variety of behaviour disorders, sometimes of far greater significance than the fits themselves.

Diphenylhydantoin (*phenytoin*, '*dilantin*', '*epanutin*') may be tried in major convulsive, temporal lobe, and other focal epilepsy. It may produce a variety of cutaneous eruptions, acne, hirsutism and rashes. At times it will provoke ataxia. Gum hypertrophy is common.

Ethyl methyl succinamide ('*zarontin*') may be tried in various types of minor epilepsy. It is relatively safe though it may cause nausea and vomiting.

Primidone ('*mysoline*') represents an alternative to pheno-barbitone, to which it is metabolized in the body (see also

p. 129). In using this drug it may be necessary to start with fractions of the dose considered therapeutic in order to avoid such a variety of unpleasant sensations that the patient may not willingly accept it again.

Ethotoin ('*peganone*') is an alternative to 'epanutin' and may be less likely to produce cutaneous changes.

Diazepines have recently come into favour. The strictly anticonvulsant property of chlordiazepoxide ('librium') is arguable. It may have some effect through control of anxiety and overactivity.

Diazepam ('*valium*') has rapidly won favour in the control of status epilepticus. The advantages are that small injections can be given intravenously, a large percentage of attacks of status epilepticus are stopped, it does not produce deep sleep, and the unconscious patient may well rouse. This allows an early history and examination to be made and attention paid to the cause of the status. At present it deserves to be used first in this condition, followed if it fails by short-acting barbiturates.

Amphetamine. In some young children this drug reduces fit frequency and it calms severe hyperkinesis. In adults it is generally stimulating and is used as an adjunct to enliven patients already heavily sedated by phenobarbitone etc. The need for its use in this particular way may suggest the importance of a reappraisal of the whole therapeutic regime.

Diuretics are sometimes used as an adjunct to therapy especially when the frequency of attacks is clearly related to a phase of the menstrual cycle.

There are few conditions other than epilepsy in which drugs are used to modify cerebral activity over a period of many years. Drugs which affect behaviour, unlike replacement therapies or specific organ therapies, cannot be readily titrated against effect. They stand in sharp contrast to the diuretics just mentioned. Behaviour is very difficult to measure and its variability with drug treatment is easily overlooked. Performance may be impaired at a point far short of intoxication.

Drugs which affect behaviour may not have a linear dose-response curve. Excessive medication may in fact promote a langour in which fits increase. Nor need the drugs have a similar action on the organism at all ages and their effects may vary with the ambient mood. Patients, especially those with psychological disturbance, are extremely variable in their attitude to taking drugs and failure of simple remedies ought to provoke enquiry into whether they are actually being taken. (Joyce, 1962; see also p. 102).

This is not to say that drugs do not have a major part to play in the treatment of epilepsy but it means that they cannot be used effectively unless they are considered against the *total* effect they produce. It may prove very well worth while to sedate a patient heavily in order to control fits, but it should be the result of a considered judgment rather than of following *ad hoc* rules of posology.

SURGICAL TREATMENT

Patients with epilepsy associated with expanding intracranial lesions need referral to a neurosurgeon. The expanding lesions most capable of being overlooked are those of the right temporal lobe.

Apart from lifesaving measures surgical treatment offers to some patients the chance of a reduced incapacity. Early surgical techniques were confined to the removal of visible cortical scars the location of which could be deduced clinically. With sophistication of electroencephalographic techniques the expert may be able to detect for the attacks a constant electrical focus under which may lie a structural abnormality, perhaps only evident microscopically. Where it lies in a surgically accessible area of the brain, its removal may be indicated if the patient's incapacity is severe enough. This incapacity must be weighed against the risks of surgical morbidity or post-operative psychological defect.

Failures of management as shown by uncontrolled seizures,

automatisms, disordered mood or behaviour, are most evident in epilepsy of temporal lobe which, being accessible, is most commonly operated upon. Only unilateral lobectomy is feasible because bilateral lobectomy produces a catastrophic effect similar to that seen in Klüver and Bucy's monkeys. The method of selecting cases, the indications for surgery, the rationale of the operation and the system of reporting results have been criticised. (Meyers, 1954; Bates, 1962). It is however becoming increasingly evident that surgical treatment has a role to play and that improvement following surgery is not limited merely to relief of the fits. Results are best where distinct lesions are removed.

Alternative means of modifying behaviour and fit frequency depend upon the interruption of neuronal circuits concerned in the propagation of attacks, by lobotomy, or with stereotactic lesions. Here it is feasible to operate bilaterally without producing devastating defects. Used on patients with bilateral abnormalities the operations are statistically less successful than those from lobectomy series, but of course the dysfunction is probably more diffuse.

Recently there has been new interest in total section of the corpus callosum on the hypothesis that the corpus callosum carries seizure discharges and allows their generalisation. There is as yet little evidence on which to base judgement about the success of such procedures and none as to the precise indications for them (Leader, 1966).

PSYCHOLOGICAL TREATMENT

All physicians must realise that a patient with a chronic disorder, especially a chronic cerebral disorder, has some psychological difficulties. Psychiatrists naturally tend to have referred to them patients who have mental disorder as well as epilepsy and this colours their views of the frequency of the association. On the other hand the detection of psychopathology in the patient will depend upon the skill of the therapist and the needs of the situation. The frequency with which a relationship between epilepsy and mental disorder is reported will be modified by these factors.

The existence of a severe personality disorder and rich psychopathology together with epilepsy need not imply a causal association either way. Mostly the psychiatrist will encounter epileptics who are seriously incapacitated by their chronic disorder, with powerful social overtones of distaste, disgust and demonology. Dostoievsky's choice of title for his books, 'The Idiot' and 'The Possessed' sum up society's views of epilepsy. The epileptic patient is himself a member of the society which thinks this way as well as being the victim of it. Abnormal mental reactions may originate from the same source as the primary handicap, or in reaction to the incapacity, or in reaction to the prejudice of society, or as the result of poor management by parents, school teachers or doctors (see Meeting, 1963; especially Hill, Pond, Williams).

The secondary handicaps are likely to be the more modifiable. It may be arduous and unrewarding to attempt to modify attitudes by formal psychotherapy but sound advice, trust, long-term support, and assistance with specific problems may allow a patient increasing independence from his intimates, reduce domestic friction, and limit the reinforcement of unsatisfactory mechanisms. Experience suggests that failure of motivation underlies many of the patient's difficulties. The psychiatrist may seek to mobilise the patient's resources through his relationship until external rewards can act as a more secure inducement.

Much has been written about the epileptic personality. Recently the trend has been to deny that any specific traits are constant. Nevertheless epilepsy is one basis for the organic mental reactions and for 'dissolution of high nervous activity' in the Jacksonian sense and these reactions may give the general form of the mental disorders.

The abnormal mental states associated with epilepsy may be chronic or acute. Various types of aggressive personality disorder are common and the chronic schizophreniform psychoses relatively rare. The more acute disturbances occur either as a prodrome or as part of post-ictal confusion. One factor to remember is that the frequency of convulsions and the mood may be antithetical, so that the reduction of seizures and the disappearance from the EEG record of the abnormal elements may be accompanied by a severe exacerbation of the mental disorder. Such a relationship extends from the hyperkinetic syndrome of children* to the paranoid hallucinatory states of mid-adult life. Severe depressions occurring in patients relieved of epilepsy by surgery have required ECT. At times it will be necessary to use phenothiazines and anti-depressant drugs. Chlorpromazine may lead to fluid retention and it is convulsant. These effects should be remembered, especially when medicating a patient whose mental disturbance follows an acute exacerbation of his epilepsy.

The reactions of the patient's relatives range between overwhelming solicitude with denial of the handicap and gross overestimation of capacity, to total rejection and exaggeration of the difficulties. The former attitude which has been called hyperpaedophilia may lead to severe neglect of other members of the family. The best therapeutic attitude would seem to be to demonstrate to the family that medical care allows reasonable freedom without neglecting any therapeutic opportunity. The best way of bringing the parents into the therapeutic relationship is by demonstrating that they are safe and right to trust the doctor.

SOCIAL TREATMENT

Asylum

The word asylum has been devalued into a pejorative term: the concept of asylum remains. A proportion of patients will require custodial care, some will need medical supervision, but others may find that an ordered environment with minimal assistance acts as a firmer base from which to build their future than their disordered home backgrounds provided.

*See Ounsted (1955).

Occupation

Occupation has been said to symbolise a place among the living (Wilensky). The social and economic effects of being known to be epileptic may be disastrous because a person may be unable to find work of a suitable nature or else may become unemployed, because of inability to drive or handle machines or through prejudice. Retraining through the Industrial Rehabilitation Units may prove satisfactory when it is simply a question of finding an alternative job. It is more difficult for such units to help patients who have lost their confidence and their motivation through prolonged unemployment. It may prove more useful to use occupational therapy and then hospital workshops in the early stages of this retraining.

Education

Epilepsy has its greatest incidence in childhood. Using the prevalence figures of the Isle of Wight survey (0.88% children aged 5-15) the Plowden Committee estimated that there must be 60,000 epileptic school children in Britain. There are at least a dozen ways in which epilepsy can interfere with the learning process (Ounsted). Although the I.Q. may be average or even in the superior range it is not unusual for epileptic children to perform at a level below that expected of them from their backgrounds, tested abilities, and opportunities. The frequency of spike, and spike and wave discharges (Hutt et al., 1963 and 1968) as well as the frequency of fits varies with attention and anxiety and the difficulty of the task. Although education occupies the major part of the life of the epileptic child and provides a variety of elements which could modify the frequency of fits, little is known of the effects of various types of learning or training on the eventual outcome. It is however clear that the type of education should be related to available performance rather than to a parental or scholastic ideal. Therapeutic intervention includes appropriate educational placement.

The management of learning disorders in epileptic children is a matter which will need considerable further research.

REFERENCES

BATES J. A. V. (1962) The surgery of epilepsy in *Modern Trends in Neurology*, 3, Ed. D. Williams, Butterworth, London.

DOMINIAN J., SERAFETINIDES E. A. and DEWHURST M. (1963) A follow-up study of late onset epilepsy. II. Psychiatric and social findings. *Brit. med. J.*, 1, 431.

EARLE K. M., BALDWIN M. and PENFIELD W. (1953) Incisural sclerosis and temporal lobe seizures produced by hippocampal herniation at birth. *Arch. Neuerol. Psychiat.*, 69, 27.

FALCONER M. A., SERAFETINIDES E. A. and CORSELLIS J. A. N. (1964) Etiology and pathogenesis of temporal lobe epilepsy. *Arch Neurol.*, 10, 233.

FALCONER M. A. and TAYLOR D. C. (1968) Surgical treatment of drug resistant temporal lobe epilepsy due to mesial temporal sclerosis. *Arch. Neurol.*, 19, 353.

GASTAUT H. (1953) So-called psychomotor and temporal lobe epilepsy. *Epilepsia*, 2, 59.

HUTT S. J. and LEE D. (1968) Some determinants of an amnesic phenomenon in a light-sensitive epileptic child. *J. neurol. Sci.*, 6, 155.

HUTT S. J., LEE D. and OUNSTED C. (1963) Digit memory and evoked discharges in four light-sensitive epileptic children. *Develop. Med. Child Neurol.*, 5, 559.

JOYCE C. R. B. (1962) Patient co-operation and the sensitivity of clinical trials. *J. chron. Dis.*, 15, 1025.

LEADER (1966) Split Brains. *Lancet*, 2, 1117.

MEETING (1963) Maturation, epilepsy and psychiatry. *Proc. Roy. Soc. Med.*, 56, 707.

MEYERS R. (1954) The surgical treatment of focal epilepsy. *Epilepsia*, 3, 1.

OUNSTED C. (1955) The hyperkinetic syndrome in epileptic children. *Lancet*, 2, 303.

OUNSTED C., LINDSAY J. and NORMAN R. (1966) Biological factors in temporal lobe epilepsy, *Clinics in Developmental Medicine, No. 22.* Heineman, London.

TAYLOR D. C. and FALCONER M. A. (1968) Clinical, socio-economic and psychological adjustment after temporal lobectomy for epilepsy. *Brit. J. Psychiat.* 114, 1247.

TODAY'S DRUGS (1968) Drug treatment of epilepsy. *Brit. med. J.*, 2, 350.

WILLIAMS D. (1956) The structure of emotions reflected in epileptic experience, *Brain*, 79, 29.

Drug Metabolism

D. V. PARKE
University of Surrey,
London.

The current widespread interest in drug metabolism is most probably due to an appreciation that the metabolic fate of a drug often determines the intensity and duration of its pharmacological activity and therapeutic use, and may explain phenomena of drug interaction (incompatibility) and drug toxicity. In modern methods of chemotherapy multiple prescription and polypharmacy are commonplace, and prolonged treatment with drugs is usual in the management of chronic diseases such as diabetes, hypertension and thrombosis. In no branch of medicine is this more true than in psychiatry, where patients are maintained for long periods and often indefinitely on a variety of barbiturates, phenothiazines etc.

Drugs like other toxic and selectively-toxic chemicals such as pesticides and food additives are metabolized in the body by a number of enzyme systems, the normal role of which is to protect the individual against the toxic effects of the naturally-occurring anutrients present in the diet (Parke, 1968). One consequence of this is that drugs will compete with dietary anutrients for metabolism, and prolonged treatment with one drug will have profound effects on the metabolism of other drugs, and of other toxic chemicals, including substances normally present in food or in the environment.

Effects of metabolism on drug activity

The metabolism of a drug usually leads to an increase of polarity of the molecule, to a decrease in its lipid-solubility, and to a more rapid elimination from the body. This is usually accompanied by a loss of pharmacological activity and by a decrease in toxicity (see Table 1), but probably because most drugs are unnatural substrates of the enzymes that metabolize them this is not always the case. Many instances are known where metabolism results not in a loss of pharmacological activity (deactivation) but instead gives rise to a gain of activity (activation), to a change of type of activity, or even to an increase in toxicity (intoxication) (see Table 2).

TABLE 1. Metabolic deactivation of drugs.

Drug	Metabolic reaction	Product	Activity lost
Adrenaline	O-methylation	3-0-methyladrenaline	Stimulant
Phenobarbitone	aromatic hydroxylation	p-hydroxyphenobarbitone	Sedative
Meprobamate	acyclic hydroxylation	hydroxymeprobamate	Tranquillizer
Mescaline	oxidative deamination	3,4,5,-trimethoxy-phenylacetic acid	Hallucinogen
Chlorpromazine	N-demethylation	desmethylchlorpromazine	Tranquillizer

In these cases where the initial products of metabolism are pharmacologically more active, of a different activity, or more toxic, further metabolism usually occurs which deactivates the molecule and facilitates its excretion. The psychostimulant-antidepressive drug imipramine may serve as example. The active principle appears to be a metabolite of imipramine, desmethylimipramine, rather than the drug itself. The metabolite is eventually deactivated either to a small extent by further metabolism involving demethylation to desdimethylimipramine,

TABLE 2. Metabolic changes in activity of drugs

Drug	Metabolic reaction	Product	Change in Activity
Codeine	O-demethylation	morphine	Analgesic⟶ Narcotic
Iproniazid	N-dealkylation	isoniazid	Antidepressive⟶ Antitubercular
Primidone	alicyclic oxidation	phenobarbitone	Anticonvulsant⟶ Sedative
Phenacetin	deacetylation	p-phenetidine	Analgesic⟶ Methaemoglobin-former (intoxicant)

or mostly by hydroxylation of the aromatic ring to give 2-hydroxydesmethylimipramine which is finally conjugated with glucuronic acid and excreted (Dingell, *et al*, 1964).

Imipramine

N-demethylation

aromatic hydroxylation

Desmethylimipramine (active drug)

glucuronide conjugation

2-Hydroxydesmethylimipramine glucuronide (inactive conjugate)

2-Hydroxydesmethylimipramine (inactive metabolite)

TABLE 3. Metabolic transformation of drugs

Reaction	Cellular Enzyme site	Biotransformations	Drug	Metabolite
OXIDATIONS:				
Aromatic hydroxylation	Endoplasmic reticulum	$C_6H_5X \rightarrow C_6H_4 \genfrac{}{}{0pt}{}{OH}{X}$	Phenobarbital	p-Hydroxyphenobarbital
Acyclic hydroxylation	Endoplasmic reticulum	$RCH_3 \rightarrow RCH_2OH$	Meprobamate	Hydroxymeprobamate
Dealkylation	Endoplasmic reticulum	$-N\genfrac{}{}{0pt}{}{CH_3}{CH_3} \rightarrow -N\genfrac{}{}{0pt}{}{H}{CH_3}$	Imipramine	Desmethylimipramine
Deamination	Endoplasmic reticulum	$\genfrac{}{}{0pt}{}{R}{R_1}CHNH_2 \rightarrow \genfrac{}{}{0pt}{}{R}{R_1}CO$	Amphetamine	Benzylmethyl ketone
Sulphoxidation	Endoplasmic reticulum	$\genfrac{}{}{0pt}{}{R}{R_1}S \rightarrow \genfrac{}{}{0pt}{}{R}{R_1}SO$	Thioridazine	Sulphoxides
N-Oxidation	Endoplasmic reticulum	$NR(CH_3)_2 \rightarrow \overset{O}{\underset{\uparrow}{R}}N(CH_3)_2$	Chlorpromazine	Chlorpromazine N-oxide
Desulphuration	Endoplasmic reticulum	$>C=S \rightarrow >C=O$	Thiobarbital	Barbital
Acyclic oxidation	Soluble fraction	$RCHO \rightarrow RCOOH$	Chloral hydrate	Trichloroacetic acid
Deamination	Mitochondria	$RCH_2NH_2 \rightarrow RCHO$	Noradrenaline	3,4-Dihydroxymandelic acid

REDUCTIONS:				
Reduction of nitro compounds	Endoplasmic reticulum/soluble fraction	$RNO_2 \rightarrow RNH_2$	Chloramphenicol	Primary amines
Reductive scission	Endoplasmic reticulum	$RN=NR \rightarrow 2RNH_2$	Prontosil	Sulphanilamide
Dehydroxylation	Intestinal microflora	$ROH \rightarrow RH$	Noradrenaline	m-Hydroxy phenylacetic acid
HYDROLYSES:				
Hydrolysis of esters	Blood plasma Hepatic cells	$RCOOR_1 \rightarrow RCOOH + R_1OH$	Meperidine	Meperidinic acid + ethanol
Hydrolysis of amides	Blood plasma	$RCONH_2 \rightarrow RCOOH + NH_2$	Procaine amide	p-Aminobenzoic acid + Diethyl ethylenediamine

TABLE 4. Conjugation of drugs and their metabolites

Conjugation	Coenzyme	Synthesis	Drug or metabolite	Conjugate
Glucuronide formation	uridine diphosphate glucuronic acid	$ROH \rightarrow RO.C_6H_9O_6$	hydroxymeprobamate	hydroxymeprobamate O-glucuronide
,,	,,	$RNH_2 \rightarrow RNH.C_6H_9O_6$	meprobamate	meprobamate N-glucuronide
Sulphate ester formation	3-phosphoadenosine-5-phosphosulphate (PAPS)	$ROH \rightarrow RO.SO_3H$	hydroxychlorpromazine	hydroxychlorpromazine sulphate
Methylation	5-adenosylmethionine	$ROH \rightarrow ROCH_3$	adrenaline	metanephrine
Acetylation	acetyl coenzyme A	$RNH_2 \rightarrow RNHCOCH_3$	mescaline	N-acetylmescaline
Peptide formation	acyl coenzyme A	$RCOOH \rightarrow RCONHCH_2COOH$	p-aminosalicylic acid	p-aminosalicyluric acid
Mercapturic acid formation	glutathione	$RH \rightarrow R-SCH_2CH(COOH)NHCOCH_3$	Phenacetin	p-acetamidophenyl mercapturic acid

Pathways of metabolism

The metabolism of drugs involves two types or stages of reaction, namely *metabolic transformation* and *conjugation*. A drug may be metabolized by one or both types of reaction, but normally transformation occurs first.

Metabolic transformations are enzymic reactions in which drugs are chemically transformed by the introduction of new functional groups into the molecule or by the removal of existing ones. They include a variety of oxidations, reductions, and hydro-lyses and often result in an increase of polarity (and water-solubility) of the molecule (see Table 3). The new functional groups may serve as centres for conjugation.

Conjugations are biosyntheses in which the drug, or any of its metabolites, are combined with one of a number of endogenous substrates, such as glucuronic acid, sulphate, amino acids, or acetyl or methyl groups, making the molecule more polar, less lipid-soluble, and more readily excreted. These endogenous substrates are transferred from coenzymes normally concerned in the intermediary metabolism of nutrients (see Table 4).

With a complex drug that possesses several different functional groups many possible alternative routes of metabolism will be available and the number of metabolites and conjugates will be large. Chlorpromazine, for example, may in principle give rise to more than one hundred different metabolic products (viz. Coccia and Westerfeld, 1967).

Many of the metabolic transformation reactions and some of the conjugations (glucuronide formation) are catalysed by enzymes present in the endoplasmic reticulum (microsomes) of the hepatic cells of the liver. These enzymes are hence known as the 'hepatic microsomal drug-metabolizing enzymes'. Other enzymes are located in the mitochondria, e.g. monoamine oxidase and the enzymes involved in peptide formation, or in the cell-sap (soluble fraction), e.g. the enzymes concerned in the reduction of nitro compounds and in the formation of sulphate esters.

Chlorpromazine

Metabolic reactions	Products	No. of variants
Dealkylation	N-oxide, Desmethyl-, Desdimethyl-	(4)
Oxidative deamination	10-Propionic acid, 10-Propanol	(3)
Cleave N-10 side-chain	2-Chlorophenothiazines	(2)
Sulphoxidation	Sulphoxides, sulphones	(3)
Aromatic hydroxylation	7-, 3- and 3, 7-Hydroxy derivatives	(4)
Conjugations	Glucuronides and sulphate esters	(3)

Total possible $= 4 \times 3 \times 2 \times 3 \times 4 \times 3 = 864$.

Further enzymes are located in other tissues such as the kidneys, lungs, skin, blood plasma, and the reticuloendothelial system.

The drug and its metabolites and conjugates may be excreted in the bile as well as the urine, and so find its way into the faeces. Excretion of compounds in bile appears to be dependent on molecular size, and this route of elimination from the body becomes significant for drugs with molecular weights greater than 400. Many drugs used in psychiatry, for example the phenothiazines, have molecular weights of 300-400, while their conjugates reach 500 or more and are therefore excreted in the bile in quantity. One of the consequences of this is that the drugs and their metabolites are carried down into the duodenum and may then be reabsorbed from the intestines, possibly after attack by the intestinal microflora. They then undergo further metabolism in the liver and other tissues, and the new metabolites may again be excreted in the bile. This is the *enterohepatic circulation* of the drug and its metabolites, which means that drugs of high molecular weight undergo a complex programme of metabolism involving mammalian and bacterial enzymes acting alternately.

Factors affecting drug metabolism

The metabolism of a drug, and therefore the intensity and duration of its pharmacological activity, may be affected by a variety of factors genetic, physiological, environmental, or pharmacodynamic in origin. The toxic side-effects of drugs may also be affected. These factors are listed in Table 5 and some of the more important of them are dealt with subsequently in greater detail.

TABLE 5. Factors affecting drug metabolism

Genetic factors:	Species differences
	Individual differences in the same species.
Physiological factors:	Age
	Hormones
	Sex
	Pregnancy
	Diet
	Disease
	Nature of intestinal microflora.
Environmental factors:	Stress
	Anutrient chemicals—food additives, pesticides, carcinogens.
	Carbon monoxide.
Pharmacodynamic factors:	Competition of other drugs.

Species differences

Major differences in the mode of metabolism of drugs by different species are restricted to variations in conjugation. For example whereas mammals, birds, reptiles, and amphibia form glucuronide conjugates of phenols we find insects, molluscs, bacteria, and plants form the corresponding glucosides instead. While all terrestrial animals form glycine conjugates birds and reptiles also form conjugates with ornithine, insects give conjugates with arginine, and man and other primates form glutamine conjugates. Most species differences are relative rather than fundamental, a difference of quantitative emphasis in alternative pathways of metabolism in different species. For example amphetamine is mostly hydroxylated to p-hydroxyamphetamine in the rat, whereas in the rabbit it mostly undergoes oxidative deamination*, and in man and dog it is mostly excreted unchanged.

TABLE 6. The comparative metabolism of amphetamine

Species	Rate of excretion in the urine (% dose in 24 hr)	Excretion product (% dose)		
		amphetamine	p-hydroxy-amphetamine	deamination metabolites*
Rat	84	13	60	3
Rabbit	81	4	7	57
Man	66	30	3	23
Dog	89	38	7	37

*benzyl methyl ketone, phenylpropanol and benzoic acid (from Dring, et al, 1966).

Rates of metabolism may also vary with species and this may have profound consequences on comparative pharmacological activity. Imipramine, which has been observed to have a stimulatory action in man and rat but little or none in mouse and rabbit, is rapidly metabolized into desmethylimipramine (DMI) a pharmacologically active metabolite, by rat, rabbit and mouse, but further metabolism into the inactive desdimethylimipramine and hydroxylated derivatives is rapid only in rabbit and mouse. Thus it is only in man and the rat that high levels of the active DMI are attained, and it is only in these species that pharmacological activity is observed (Dingell, *et al.*, 1964).

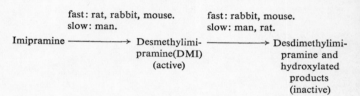

Most of the preliminary testing for the safety of new drugs is carried out with laboratory animals rather than man, and it is thus desirable to select a species for these studies in which the drug will have effects similar to those observed in man. As both the pharmacological and toxic activities of a drug may be related to its pattern of metabolism the most appropriate species would be that in which the metabolism of the drug was the most similar to that in man. A knowledge of the metabolism of a drug, and a quantitative account of its metabolic fate in different species is therefore of great importance in the production and testing of new drugs.

Individual differences

Differences in the individual pharmacological response to drugs, and the capricious appearance of toxic side-effects, may often be due to genetically-determined enzyme defects which result in variations in the rates of metabolism of drugs. The acetylation of isoniazid, sulphamezathine and the substituted hydrazine drugs, hydralazine and phenelzine ('nardil'), and hence their deactivation, may proceed at different rates in different individuals who may be 'slow' or 'fast' deactivators. Slow deactivators treated with isoniazid exhibit peripheral neuropathies many times more frequently than do the fast deactivators. Similar genetic variations are known to occur with other drug-metabolizing enzymes, for example plasma pseudocholinesterase, an enzyme that deactivates esters such as the anaesthetic, procaine, and the muscle-relaxant, succinylcholine.

Age

Neonates of all species have a limited capacity to metabolize drugs, which makes them particularly vulnerable to any toxic effects. This is because many of the enzyme systems responsible for the metabolism of drugs do not develop until after birth. In the rat the acute toxicities of many drugs (not amphetamine) is much greater in the newborn animal than in the adult (Yeary, *et al.*, 1966).

TABLE 7. Acute toxicities of drugs in the new-born rat

| Drug | Oral LD_{50} (mg./kg.) | |
	Newborn (1-3 days old)	Adult
Dicoumarin	70	700
Paracetamol	420	2400
Meprobamate	350	1500
Phenobarbital	120	320
Desipramine HCl	130	320
d-Amphetamine	80	40

(from Yeary, *et al*, 1966).

Pregnancy

It has long been accepted practice that the administration of drugs during pregnancy is undesirable, probably because it is known that many drugs may cross the placental barrier and consequently affect the foetus, e.g. imipramine has shown to undergo rapid placental transfer, equilibrium between the maternal and foetal systems being established within minutes (Douglas and Hume, 1967). It has also been shown that the metabolism of several drugs including phenacetin, aminopyrine and pethidine is inhibited during pregnancy (Creaven and Parke, 1965; Crawford and Rudofsky, 1966).

The progestational steroids used as oral contraceptives may give rise to an inhibition of drug metabolism similar to that observed in pregnancy (Juchau and Fouts, 1966). An illustration of the possible effects of these contraceptive steroids on the metabolism and activity of drugs is given in a case reported by Keeler and his co-workers (1964) concerning a female patient suffering from schizophrenia, who having previously received norethynodrel-mestranol for suspected endometriosis was treated with chlorpromazine. After two weeks the patient was restarted on norethynodrel-mestranol and the psychotic manifestations began to diminish, but on withdrawal of the norethynodrel-mestranol the psychotic symptoms reappeared. One explanation of these observations would be that an initial stimulation of the metabolism of the chlorpromazine was induced by the previous treatment with the oral contraceptive, and that this was followed by an inhibitory effect on the metabolism when the oral contraceptive was readministered. A second period of stimulation followed the subsequent withdrawal of the norethynodrel.

Stress

Under conditions of stress the metabolism of drugs is stimulated, and blood levels of drugs such as hexobarbital, pentobarbital and meprobamate have been found to be significantly lower in stressed than in normal animals (Driever and Bousquet, 1965). This stimulation of drug metabolism by stress is dependent upon the pituitary-adrenal axis and is probably the result of induction of microsomal drug-metabolizing enzymes by the adrenal corticosteroid hormones.

Anutrient chemicals

A similar induction of the microsomal drug-metabolizing enzymes is produced by many chemical substances other than corticosteroids. These are all anutrient compounds, and include pesticides, food additives, carcinogens, and of course, drugs themselves. The ability to stimulate the formation of additional drug-metabolizing enzymes is quite unrelated to the pharmacological or toxic activities of the inducing compounds, and may be due primarily to the extent to which the compound binds with histones to remove the repressing effect of these proteins on the cellular control of enzyme synthesis. Compounds which have been shown to stimulate drug metabolism include DDT and chlordane (pesticides), butylated hydroxytoluene (food additive), coumarins and terpenes (natural substances), benzpyrene and methylcholanthrene (carcinogens) and barbiturates, phenothiazines and meprobamate.

These stimulatory effects of anutrient chemicals on the metabolism of drugs, and even the self-stimulation by drugs of

TABLE 8. Stimulation of drug metabolism by pretreatment with drugs

	Level of metabolism of:		
Pretreatment	Hexobarbital (% normal)	Aminopyrine (% normal)	Meprobamate (% normal)
Phenobarbital	270	300	260
Glutethimide	190	200	200
Chlorpromazine	140	160	150
Carisoprodol	140	145	160

their own metabolism, may greatly reduce the circulating levels of drugs, their duration of action and their therapeutic effect. After a single dose of any of these compounds the stimulatory effects on drug metabolism last for several days, but with chronic administration the effects may persist for several months after treatment has ceased. The development of tolerance to barbiturates, meprobamate and other drugs is no doubt due to the stimulatory action that these drugs have on their own metabolism.

The interaction of drugs that result from this kind of stimulation are numerous and well documented (Conney, 1967), but observations of clinical phenomena resulting from the effects of pesticides, food additives, etc. on drug metabolism are relatively few. Chronic administration of phenobarbitone in conjunction with diphenylhydantoin ('dilantin') in the treatment of epilepsy reduces the anticonvulsant effect of the latter drug, and in conjunction with bishydroxycoumarin (dicoumarol) in the treatment of thrombosis it reduces the anticoagulant activity.

The simultaneous administration of chloral hydrate has also been shown to stimulate the metabolism of bishydroxycoumarin, and when chloral hydrate was discontinued in a patient also receiving bishydroxycoumarin the prothrombin time increased and a fatal haemorrhage occurred. These examples serve to illustrate the clinical importance of the stimulatory effects of drugs and environmental chemicals on the metabolism of drugs.

Pharmacodynamic effects

Drugs, environmental chemicals and steroids are all metabolized by the same microsomal drug-metabolizing enzymes, so that when any of these different substrates are presented simultaneously to the enzymes a competition for the enzyme occurs. Thus the metabolism of drug A may be inhibited by the simultaneous metabolism of another drug B, and this means that A shows a prolonged activity.

This inhibitory action on drug metabolism is exhibited by

most drugs, and is not incompatible with their stimulatory action previously described. The initial effect is always one of competitive enzymic inhibition for four to twelve hours, which is then usually followed by induction of the microsomal enzymes and a period of enzymic stimulation, lasting a few days or longer. Thus pharmacologically and clinically there should be a flare-up of activity, and then a decrease. Morphine and other related narcotics are unusual in that they inhibit the metabolism of other drugs but show no subsequent phase of metabolic stimulation.

A knowledge of the competitive inhibition by one drug of the metabolism of another and of its potential synergism of action is particularly important when dosage is being considered in multiple prescriptions or polypharmacy. Moreover, because of the biphasic nature of inhibition and stimulation, contrasting effects may be observed by varying the time interval between the administration of the drug and its synergist.

Phenyramidol, an intraneuronal blocking agent, increases the anticoagulant activity of several coumarin derivatives such as bishydroxycoumarin by inhibition of their metabolism, so that the usual therapeutic dose of the anticoagulants becomes excessive and spontaneous haemorrhage may occur (Solomon and Schrogie, 1966). Similarly, it has been observed that epileptic patients poorly controlled on diphenylhydantoin ('epanutin') improved following the introduction of phenyramidol to the therapeutic regimen (Solomon and Schrogie, 1967). Desmethylimipramine inhibits the metabolism of amphetamine and other drugs (Sulser, et al., 1966), and 'antabuse', the anti-alcoholism drug, inhibits the metabolism of diphenylhydantoin (Olesen, 1966).

Drug synergism may also arise from the competition of drugs for binding sites on plasma proteins. Drugs such as the sulphonamides, salicyclic acid and phenylbutazone which are strong binders to protein displace other less strongly bound drugs from their binding sites on plasma proteins, resulting in higher free and tissue levels of the latter and enhanced pharmacological activity.

The oral administration of some drugs may also affect the rate of absorption of other drugs. Amphetamine has been shown to retard the absorption from the gut of phenobarbital and diphenylhydantoin and to delay their anticonvulsant action (Frey and Kampmann, 1966).

The extent of metabolism may also be affected by the rate of excretion of the unchanged drug in the urine, which in turn may be dependent on the pH of the urine. For example the rate of excretion of the basic drug amphetamine was twenty times greater in human subjects with urine of pH 5 than in others with urine of pH 8 (Beckett, *et al.*, 1965). Therefore in patients with an acid urine amphetamine will be more rapidly excreted, less pharmacologically potent, and less extensively metabolized than in those with a neutral or alkaline urine.

We are still only at the beginning of understanding all these factors influencing drug actions. They are likely to be especially important in psychiatry where drugs in different combinations are often given over very long periods.

REFERENCES

BECKETT A. H., ROWLAND M. and TURNER P. (1965) *Lancet*, *I*. 303.

COCCIA P. F. and WESTERFELD W. W. (1967) *J. Pharm. Exp. Therap.*, **157**, 446-58

CONNEY A. H. (1967) *Pharmacol. Rev.*., **3**, 317-66.

CRAWFORD J. S. and RUDOFSKY S. (1966) *Brit J. Anaesth.*, **38**, 446-54.

CREAVEN P. J. and PARKE D. V. (1965) *Fed. Europ. Biochem. Soc. 2nd. Meeting Abstr.*, A128, pp. 88-89.

DINGELL J. V., SULSER F. and GILLETTE J. R. (1964) *J. Pharmac. Exp.. Therap.*, **143**, 14-22.

DOUGLAS B. H. and HUME A. D. (1967) *Am. J. Obstetr. Gynaec.*, **99**, 573-5.

DRIEVER C. W. and BOUSQUET W. F. (1965) *Life Sciences*, **4**, 1449-54.

DRING L. G., SMITH R. L. and WILLIAMS R. T. (1966) *J. Pharm. Pharmac.*, **18**, 402-5.

FREY H. H. and KAMPMANN E. (1966) *Acta Pharmac. Toxicol.*, **24**, 310-16.

JUCHAU M. R. and FOUTS J. R. (1966) *Biochem. Pharmac.*, **15**, 891-8.

KEELER M. H., KANE F. and DALY R. (1964) *Am. J. Psychiat.*, **120**, 1123-4.

OLESEN O. V. (1966) *Acta Pharmac. Toxicol.*, **24**, 317-22.

PARKE D. V. (1968) *The Biochemistry of Foreign Compounds*, Pergamon Press, Oxford.

SOLOMON H. M. and SCHROGIE J. J. (1966) *J. Pharmac. Exp. Therap.* **154**, 660-6.

SOLOMON H. M. and SCHROGIE J. J. (1967) *Clin. Pharmac. Therap.*, **8**, 554-6.

SULSER F., OWENS M. L. and DINGELL J. V. (1966) *Life Sciences*, **5**, 2005-10.

YEARY R. A., BENISH R. A. and FINKELSTEIN M. (1966) *J. Pediat.*, **69**, 663-7.

Some Aspects of Clinical Trials in Psychiatry

MICHAEL SHEPHERD

Institute of Psychiatry,
Maudesley Hospital
London

I have been asked to discuss three different aspects of the therapeutic trial in the field of psychiatry: (1) the various types of trial available; (2) the necessity for them; and (3) the resources required and difficulties experienced. I shall take for granted a familiarity with the basic principles of the trial procedures which have been very clearly described elsewhere by Letemendia [1]. Most of what I have to say will be concerned with pharmacotherapy. The general principles of clinical evaluation apply also to psychological and social treatments but space is too limited for me to consider the special problems raised by these methods.

TYPES OF CLINICAL TRIAL

Doll's definition of a clinical trial, 'an experiment carried out with the object of seeing whether a treatment has any effect on the course of a disease', is as good as any and shorter than most.

It is, however, necessary to recognise that a clinical trial of a new remedy must be sub-divided into stages. A recent W.H.O. report [2] usefully suggests three phases of study. In the first phase the effective dose range, side effects and possible toxic properties of a new drug are determined: no control groups are required for this work which is usually carried out on groups of five to ten patients by enthusiastic investigators with considerable experience of drug research in human beings. In the second

145

phase the therapeutic range and effectiveness of the drug are both studied: clinical experiments in the second phase may or may not be controlled and are usually carried out with groups of between ten and thirty cases, ideally by clinicians who are able to take advantage of experience and intuition. Only in the third phase are attempts made to validate the observations already made in earlier phases by strictly controlled techniques. There are several possible designs in phase three. A new drug can be compared with no treatment, or with another drug, in an experiment which can be non-blind, single blind or double blind; alternatively, the new drug can be compared with a placebo using the single or double blind method.

There is a place for all these types of investigation, although it is often mistakenly assumed that only a comparison of drug with placebo in a double blind situation qualifies as a reputable clinical trial. The earlier phases of evaluation have been particularly neglected, as will be discussed later in this paper.

JUSTIFICATIONS FOR CLINICAL TRIALS

It remains surprisingly true that many workers can still be antagonistic to the notion of carrying out clinical experiments with substances which are potentially toxic and which can be so easily misapplied. Commenting on the heat engendered by arguments on this topic Modell has advocated an 'antipyretic' approach to the subject. In general there seem to be four principal grounds on which the notion of therapeutic trials in psychiatry have been attacked: the clinical, the ethical, the statistical and the biological. It is worth looking at representatives of these objections in turn. Each one is followed by an appropriate reply from Sir Austin Bradford Hill who has played so important a part in developing the modern clinical trial as a method of investigation.

(a) *The clinical justification*

In 1965 a multi-centred trial of treatments for depressive illness was published under the auspices of the Medical Research Council [3]. It remains the largest and probably the best organised study in the field of clinical psychiatry so far available. Nonetheless, it attracted the following comment from a prominent clinician: 'There is no psychiatric illness in which bedside knowledge and long clinical experience pays better dividends and we are never going to learn how to treat depression properly from double-blind sampling in an M.R.C. statistician's office' [4].

Bradford Hill has replied directly to this reaction, which is all too common among clinicians, in the following terms: 'Unfortunately, as one of the patients in the bed I feel more than a trifle depressed while—partly at my expense—he gains his knowledge and his long clinical experience. I would have hoped that the process of learning might be a little less long if it were supported by the experimental method and attitude of mind . . . . The statistician's office, needless to say, merely provides an experimental design upon which to hang the skilled clinical observation that must characterise *any* form of enquiry into therapeutic efficacy. There is no question of replacing valuable clinical observations by a series of mathematical symbols. Those who think so have the myopia of Don Quixote: they mistake the scaffold for the house'. [5].

(b) *The ethical justification*

Ethical reasons are also advanced by some clinicians when they are trying to avoid the use of controlled therapeutic experiments. A characteristic example may be taken from the current vogue for the supposedly prophylactic use of lithium carbonate in the management of depressive illnesses. The authors of the key paper advocating this practice write as follows: 'Since a striking prophylactic action of lithium became apparent with the first patients studied, it would have been difficult as well as painful to distribute the patients into two groups, one to receive lithium and one to be given placebo or the traditional, and in most cases rather ineffective, therapy. Since prophylactic rather than therapeutic effects were studied the patients—many of them severely handicapped by frequent relapses—would have had to remain in their group for a number of years' [6].

The impartial observer, finding that the published evidence in favour of this prophylactic action is less impressive [7], will do well to recall with Bradford Hill that '. . . medical literature abounds with examples to show that the belief that an unproved treatment (new or old) *must* for ethical reasons be exhibited is unwarranted. Some treatments are valueless, some are hazardous. The whole question is how best can we discover those facts. If the clinical trial is the method of choice then the question becomes in what circumstances can the doctor withhold (or give) a treatment while preserving the high ethical standards demanded of his profession?' [8].

While each case must be treated on its merits the six questions posed by Bradford Hill can profitably be asked by every investigator concerned with the problems of therapeutic evaluation. Is the proposed treatment safe or, in other words, is it likely to do harm to the patient? Can a new treatment be ethically withheld from a new patient in the doctor's care? What patients may be brought into a controlled trial and allocated randomly to different treatments? Is it necessary to obtain the patient's consent to his inclusion in a controlled trial? Is it ethical to use a placebo or dummy treatment? Is it proper for the doctor not to know the treatment being administered to his patient?

(c) *The statistical justification*

Several statistically sophisticated observers have raised objections to the clinical trial, most of them echoing the arguments of Claude Bernard a century ago: 'By destroying the biological character of phenomena, the use of *averages* in physiology and medicine usually gives only apparent accuracy to the results. I am unable to understand why results taken from statistics are called *laws;* for in my opinion scientific laws can be based only on certainty, on absolute determinism, not on probability' [9].

Again Bradford Hill has taken up this vexed question of the individual and the group response in respect of the well-known comparison between aspirin and cortisone in the treatment of rheumatoid arthritis: 'It (the controlled trial) may be so constituted as to show without any doubt that treatment A is *on the average* better than treatment B. On the other hand, that result does not answer the practising doctor's question what is the most likely outcome when this drug is given to a particular patient? What we found was remarkably little to choose between cortisone and aspirin in the management of this group of patients. The operative word is 'group'.

There is, of course, no suggestion that aspirin could have supplanted cortisone (or vice versa) in *all* cases and no such inference could possibly be warranted. Nevertheless, does not the finding give useful advice to the doctor faced with the individual patient? His first ambition, no doubt, will be to maintain the patient's health and well-being on no drugs at all (ethically the trial could have no such group). If that venture fails then he knows from the trial that he has two medicaments to which he can turn and that *on the average* one has shown no superiority over the other. Doubtless he will first select the one that is likely to produce the fewest adverse reactions. If that fails then he turns to the alternative. I submit that this is not a trivial contribution to his task' [5].

(d) *The biological justification*

The biologist's mistrust of statistical reasoning also extends into procedural features of the clinical trial. The major objection has been clearly illustrated by an American pharmacologist commenting on the M.R.C. trial of treatments for depression: 'Set dosage schedules of drugs are to be deplored by the biological scientist since they take into account neither patient-weight nor the wide biochemical variability in man which has been so clearly established in the past few years' [10].

Once more, Bradford Hill has provided a comprehensive answer to this view: 'In the great majority of controlled clinical trials with which I have been associated, a specific treatment schedule has always been laid down. It may, needless to say, be varied with age or body weight or some other characteristic of the patient, but apart from that it has been rigidly defined in advance and must be adhered to by the clinician (except for the usual over-riding ethical reasons). Clearly, however, in regard to treatment there are an infinite number of questions we can ask of a trial. We can choose one dose out of many; we can vary the interval of administration; we can give it by different routes; we can exhibit it for different lengths of time; and so on. In testing a new form of treatment knowledge at first is necessarily scanty, being usually based upon laboratory work and a few scattered clinical observations. In Medical Research Council trials we have thought it proper therefore to choose such a regime as promised to reveal the potentialities (and often the dangers) of a drug (or whatever may be concerned). Thus we have a tidy question—for example, if to a defined type of patient 2 gm. of drug X are given daily in four divided doses by intramuscular injection and for three months what happens?

But perhaps the question is too tidy. We can of course extend it after the answer has been reached by experimenting with variations on the original theme. It may, however, be argued, and sometimes I think, legitimately, that allowance should have been made during the basic trial for individual idiosyncrasies, that the clinician should have been free to vary the dosage according to his own judgement of the patient's needs as shown by the latter's responses. Statistically, I see no reason why that should not be done as long as two things are observed and remembered. The first is that we have deliberately changed the question asked of the trial; it now runs 'if competent clinicians in charge of defined types of patients use drug X in such varying amounts and for such varying durations of time, and so forth, as they think advisable for each patient, what happens?' The moot point is which question in given circumstances, is the better one to ask. The second point is that at the conclusion of such trials we can *in no circumstances* compare the effects of the different regimes of treatment that have been used. These regimes have been determined by the conditions and responses of individual patients; to observe then, at the end of the trial, the patient's differential conditions and responses in relation to their treatment, is no more than circular reasoning. We cannot possibly measure thus the advantages and disadvantages of different regimes but only by an expansion of the controlled trial by including groups randomly allocated to such treatments' [11].

RESOURCES REQUIRED AND DIFFICULTIES ENCOUNTERED

Many practical aspects of clinical trials in psychiatry have been insufficiently studied, particularly in the early stages of evaluation (phases 1 and 2). Who is to undertake this work and how is it done? Even when animal pharmacologists and toxicologists have determined dose-ranges and collected data on absorption, metabolism, and excretion of the drug in infra-human species [12] the extrapolation of these results to man in the case of new psychotropic drugs has been aptly called a 'leap in the dark'. With these substances the logical sequence of animal studies, testing in normal man and clinical application can rarely be followed. The Committee on Safety of Drugs is not constituted to deal with the many problems posed by the early testing of new drugs in man. Its three sub-committees—on toxicity, on adverse reactions and on clinical trials and therapeutic efficacy—are primarily concerned with questions of safety and not with the practice and organisation of early evaluation. Psychiatry is not the only branch of medicine which lacks testing centres and adequately trained workers to undertake this specialized task but at the present time the deficiency has been cruelly exposed by the mounting flood of new psychotropic preparations.

To try and make some contribution to this neglected but important area a committee was set up at the Institute of Psychiatry in 1966 to study the basic principles involved and to work out an acceptable drug trial procedure. The first investigation under these auspices has been fully reported [13] and some of the details are worth emphasising in this context. The work was centred on a new drug which had undergone animal tests, and had been passed by the Committee on Safety of Drugs for human testing subject to certain restrictions. Thus women of child-bearing age were to be excluded, as were patients exposed to recent treatment with monoamine oxidase inhibitors or any form of current anti-hypertensive treatment; extensive laboratory tests were to be made at least once a week in all trial patients. The trials were not to embrace more than a total of 30 patients, 10 for each investigator; the dose was fixed and no patient was to be exposed to the drug for more than 8 weeks. Our own aims were (a) to test under double-blind conditions whether the drug given orally to in-patients with depression had any anti-depressant or tranquillizing effects, (b) to assess the side-effects of the drug, and in doing so (c) to construct a model for testing a new anti-depressant on a restricted number of patients before its release for large scale trials.

It was found that in addition to laboratory facilities three workers were needed to prosecute this study: a full-time co-ordinator and two part-time doctors of senior registrar status who assisted with the ratings of the patients. The co-ordinator had to explain the purpose of the trial and obtain consent from patients and relatives, a crucial and very delicate matter with a new drug. He had to instruct the patients and nursing staff in completing the rating scales, and to supervise the continuous monitoring of all admissions to the hospital in order to avoid missing suitable patients. He had to be constantly available to handle inquiries concerning side-effects, collection of specimens, and completion of rating scales. Any complaint by a patient receiving a new drug must be taken seriously and the co-ordinator found it important to hold meetings for the ward staff who might tend to become concerned about the responsibility attendant on a study of this type.

During the 18 weeks of this study 518 patients were admitted to the hospital. Strict criteria for inclusion were adopted to ensure homogeneity of the patient population and accounted in part for the difficulty in obtaining suitable patients. Nonetheless, though 90 depressed patients were originally deemed suitable most had to be excluded for the following reasons: in 4 cases the patient or a relative refused consent, in 7 cases a complicating physical condition precluded use of the drug, in 9 cases recovery was so rapid that treatment could not be initiated, in 15 cases the illness was too severe and in 7 cases it was too chronic, in 21 cases there was a history of failure to respond to a similar drug, in 17 cases the responsible consultant refused consent, in 2 cases the trial procedure had to be abandoned for administrative reasons and in 2 more cases because of medical reasons. In sum, only 6 patients, i.e. 1.2% of the total number screened, or 7% of the total number of depressed patients regarded as potentially suitable, completed the trial. These figures may be taken as an index of how difficult it can be to conduct successful clinical experiments of this type even with potentially adequate resources.

Only after phases 1 and 2 of the clinical trial have been completed is it possible to tackle phase 3, the experimental validation of observations about the drug's effectiveness and side-effects. Usually this is in the form of a comparison with another treatment carried out on a group of human beings who are inevitably heterogeneous in some respects. The trial design therefore employs the statistical approach developed nearly fifty years ago by R. A. Fisher for use in biological research. Three principles are basic to all such studies. First, the random allocation of patients to the treatment under consideration makes it apply probability-theory to an analysis of the results. Secondly, the principle of replication, i.e. the use of many experimental units for each treatment, makes it possible to estimate the random variation of individual observations and to make the experimental units more representative. Thirdly, random variability can also be reduced in the interests of homogeneity by the creation of smaller homogeneous blocks within the larger units of the experimental design.

A more detailed description of the confirmatory trial [14] is unnecessary here but mention should be made of one aspect of evaluation which looms large in the evaluation of treatments in psychiatry, namely the rating-scale [15]. In the choice and preparation of such scales it is imperative that they are truly representative of the kinds of behaviour which are appropriate to the investigation. In addition the items must be formulated and pretested to ensure (a) that they apply to the relevant sample of patients, (b) that they are clearly comprehensible and form a progressive continuum, and (c) that any combination of scales has been empirically validated before they are applied. Finally, if no appropriate scale is available and a new one cannot be scientifically constructed it is best to abandon the method altogether. Elaborate but essentially meaningless statistical procedures will never turn a blunt instrument into a knife.

I should now like to return to the Medical Research Council study of treatments in depression in order to underline some practical details which must be considered in the prosecution of a successful trial. The aim of this study was the comparative evaluation of four treatments—E.C.T., a tricyclic anti-depressant, a monoamine oxidase inhibitor, and a placebo—on hospitalized men and women aged 40-69. The subjects were defined as having depression as a primary illness with certain specified symptoms, a maximum duration of eighteen months, no adequate treatment in the previous six months and no serious physical disease.

Homogeneity in respect of these characteristics was obligatory in each of the four groups of approximately 60 patients. As there was widespread prescription by general practitioners of anti-depressant medication before patients came into hospital, and as many physicians were reluctant to keep patients in hospital for the minimum period of four weeks or to prescribe E.C.T. or placebo as a randomly chosen procedure, suitable subjects were difficult to come by. Eventually 55 doctors treating a small number of patients each at 30 different hospitals were persuaded to co-operate. To organise this enquiry a central office in the M.R.C. headquarters had to be set up, staffed by workers familiar with the administrative aspects of medical statistics, a full-time secretary, a social worker, and a highly qualified physician who gave at least one day a week to the trial for a period of more than two years.

In a study of this type the morale of participating doctors becomes very important. If their interest is to be sustained and, above all, if the quality of their recording is to be good enough for analysis they must not feel themselves on the periphery of a large mechanical operation with no investment in the progress of the inquiry. To counteract this feeling of impersonality occasional meetings are insufficient and money constitutes no adequate incentive. Personal, individual, and regular contact with the supervising physician and the social worker seems to be the answer. From these contacts it was possible to establish that some physicians preferred to receive reminders by post or telephone, others through diary cards, while another group was only happy when somebody came round to see them personally. The social worker also had to trace patients who disappeared during the follow-up period, and in the event only 16 out of 269 patients were lost.

Finally, a practical point arising out of the results of this investigation may be taken to illustrate the value of the method. About one third of patients suffering from a moderately severe depressive illness were, in the opinion of their doctors, adequately treated by no other treatment than placebo; their illness remitted and they remained well for the full study period of six months. This very striking finding provides a yardstick for comparison with the effects of other therapy. The administration of E.C.T. and one of the drugs was, in fact, associated with a superior response. By contrast the other drug, a monoamine oxidase inhibitor, demonstrated no advantage over placebo and the drug manufacturers' changing claims reflected the findings in their own way. Thus it had been originally stated: 'The consensus of clinical opinion seems to be that (the drug) has a value in endogenous depression comparable with that of E.C.T.' The manufacturers' more recent reappraisal makes no mention of E.C.T. and gives 'Psychoneurotic depression (reactive depression, atypical depression, anxiety depression, depression with hysterical or obsessive/compulsive features)' as the indication for treatment with the drug. The second claim is different, but its scientific basis is as uncertain as the first. Connoisseurs of the therapeutic scene in psychiatry will do well to take to heart T. H. Huxley's comment on the natural scientist: 'For him scepticism is the highest of duties; blind faith the one unpardonable sin'.

REFERENCES

1 LETEMENDIA F. J. J. (1962) Clinical trials in psychiatry, in *Aspects of Psychiatric Research*, Eds. D. Richter, J. M. Tanner, Lord Taylor and O. L. Zangwill. Oxford University Press, p. 384.

2 WORLD HEALTH ORGANIZATION (1967) *Research in Psychopharmacology*, Technical Report Series, No. 371. Geneva.

3 MEDICAL RESEARCH COUNCIL (1965) Report by its Clinical Committee: 'Clinical Trial of the Treatment of Depressive Illness'. *Brit. Med. J.*, I, 881.

4 SARGANT W. (1965) Correspondence, *Brit. Med. J.*, I, 1495.

5 HILL A. B. (1966) Reflections on the controlled Trial, *Ann. Rheum. Dis.*, **25**, 107.

6 BAASTRUP P. C. and SCHOU M. (1967) Lithium as a prophylactic agent, *Arch. Gen. Psychiat.*, **16**, 162.

7   BLACKWELL B. and SHEPHERD M. (1968) Prophylactic lithium: another Therapeutic Myth?, *Lancet*, I, 968.

8   HILL A. B. (1963) Medical ethics and controlled trials, *Brit. Med. J.*, I, 1045.

9   BERNARD C. *An introduction to the Study of Experimental Medicine* (translated by Green H. C.), Macmillan, New York, 1927.

10 EVERETT G. M. (1966) In *Anti-Depressant Drugs*, edited by Garattini S. and Dukes M. N. G. *Excerpta Medica Foundation* I.C.S. No. 122.

11 HILL A. B. (1962) The clinical Trial, in *Statistical Methods in Clinical and Preventive Medicine*, Livingstone, Edinburgh.

12 LAURENCE D. R. (1965) General problems of the first administration of a potential drug to man, in *Evaluation of New Drugs in Man*, Ed. E. Zaimis, Pergamon, p. 95.

13 BLACKWELL B. and SHEPHERD M. (1967) Early evaluation of psychotropic drugs in man, *Lancet*, II, 819.

14 SHEPHERD M. (1963) The evaluation of treatment in psychiatry, in *Methods of Psychiatric Research*, Eds. P. Sainsbury and N. Kreitman, Oxford University Press, p. 49.

15 WITTENBORN J. R. (1964) Comments on the selection and use of symptom rating scales for research in pharmacotherapy, in *International Review of Neurobiology*, 279.

Index

Proprietary names are printed in italics.